How to Pray for One Hour

A Step-by-Step Guide with Time Segments

McDougal & Associates

Servants of Christ and Stewards of the Mysteries of God

How to Pray for One Hour

A Step-by-Step Guide with Time Segments

by

Apostle Jackie Harewood

HOW TO PRAY FOR ONE HOUR

Published by:

McDougal & Associates
www.thepublishedword.com

McDougal & Associates is dedicated to the spreading of the Gospel of Jesus Christ to as many people as possible in the shortest time possible.

ISBN 978-1-964665-27-6

Printed in the US, the UK, Australia, and the UAE
For Worldwide Distribution

ACKNOWLEDGMENTS

First and foremost, I give all glory and honor to God, the Author and Finisher of our faith, Who has guided me through the journey of writing this book. Without His wisdom, strength, and divine inspiration, this work would not have been possible.

To my husband, Apostle David Harewood: Your unwavering support, prayers, and encouragement have been a beacon of light throughout this process. Your faith in me has strengthened my resolve to bring this vision to life.

A special thank you to my spiritual mentors who have imparted wisdom, correction, and insight, helping to shape both my personal prayer life and the framework of this book. Your dedication to the Kingdom inspires me daily.

To every reader who picks up this book with a desire to deepen their prayer life: May this guide be a tool that draws you closer to the Lord, strengthens your intercession, and ignites a passion for sustained, meaningful prayer. May this book empower you to rise up and legislate the authority granted to you, bringing transformation, power, and spiritual renewal to all who engage with it.

CONTENTS

COULD YOU NOT WATCH WITH ME ONE HOUR?
— MATTHEW 26:40, ESV

WHAT'S THIS BOOK ABOUT?

How to Pray for One Hour: A Step-by-Step Guide with Time Segments

Prayer is our divine lifeline, an intimate conversation with God that strengthens our faith and brings spiritual breakthrough, yet many believers struggle with maintaining focused, structured prayer for an extended time. *How to Pray for One Hour* offers a step-by-step guide to help you maximize your time in God's presence by breaking your prayer time into intentional segments.

This book provides a clear framework rooted in Matthew 26:40, where Jesus challenged His disciples, *"Could you not watch with me one hour?"* (ESV). It teaches you how to dedicate specific time blocks to worship, intercession, repentance, spiritual warfare, and listening to God's voice, ensuring that every moment spent in prayer is effective and powerful.

Through biblical insights, structured prayer points, and practical application, this guide empowers you to overcome distractions, deepen your connection with God, and experience a transformational prayer life. Whether you're a seasoned intercessor or just beginning to develop a habit of prayer, this book will equip you to engage in an hour of impactful, Spirit-led prayer like never before.

Are you ready to step into a new dimension of prayer?

INTRODUCTION

Prayer is one of the most powerful tools we have as believers; it is our direct connection to God, a pathway to intimacy, strength, and divine intervention, yet many struggle with sustaining prayer for extended periods, feeling unsure of what to say or how to structure their time with the Lord.

This book is designed to help you pray effectively for one hour, covering multiple subjects without losing focus or momentum. Through scriptural guidance, practical strategies, and structured prayer points, you will learn how to approach prayer with intentionality and depth.

Whether you are praying for your family, your community, doing spiritual warfare, or praying for healing or personal growth, this method will equip you to stay engaged, allowing the Holy Spirit to guide you. In Matthew 26:40, Jesus asked His disciples, *"Could you not watch with me one hour?"* (ESV). This challenge reminds us that sustained prayer is both possible and essential in our spiritual journey.

The prayers that follow are structured into 60-minute segments, each with a focus area, scripture reference, guided prayer, and a suggested activity to help you stay engaged. The guide is flexible. Feel free to adjust the time allocations or add steps that resonate with your personal prayer journey.

As you embark on this journey, may your prayer life be strengthened, your faith deepened, and your connection with God transformed. This book is not just about extending prayer time, but also about enriching your communion with the Lord.

Are you ready to step into a deeper dimension of prayer? Let us begin.

Grace & Peace
Apostle Jackie Harewood
Baton Rouge, Louisiana

— HOW TO PRAY FOR ONE HOUR —

Praise and Worship (10 Minutes): Begin by praising God for who He is and worshiping Him for His greatness.

Enter his gates with thanksgiving and his courts with praise; give thanks to him and praise his name. Psalm 100:4

Suggested Activity: Sing a worship song or speak words of adoration to God.

Thanksgiving (10 Minutes): Thank God for His blessings, provision, and faithfulness in your life.

In everything give thanks; for this is God's will for you in Christ Jesus. 1 Thessalonians 5:18, NASB

Suggested Activity: Reflect on specific things you're grateful for and express your thanks.

Confession and Repentance (10 Minutes): Confess your sins and ask for forgiveness, seeking a clean heart before God.

If we confess our sins, he is faithful and just and will forgive us our sins and purify us from all un-righteousness. 1 John 1:9

Suggested Activity: Spend time in silent prayer, asking the Holy Spirit to reveal areas where you need repentance.

Intercession (10 Minutes): Pray for others, including family, friends, church leaders, and global issues.

I urge, then, first of all, that petitions, prayers, intercession and thanksgiving be made for all people. 1 Timothy 2:1

Suggested Activity: Make a list of people and situations to pray for and lift them up to God.

Petition (10 Minutes): Bring your personal needs and desires before God, trusting Him to provide.

Do not be anxious about anything, but in every situation, by prayer and petition, with thanksgiving, present your requests to God.

Philippians 4:6

Suggested Activity: Be specific about your requests and align them with God's will.

Meditation and Listening (10 Minutes): Spend time in silence, meditating on God's Word and listening for His voice.

Be still and know that I am God. Psalm 46:10

Suggested Activity: Read a passage of scripture and reflect on its meaning, asking God to speak to you.

Closing Praise and Commitment: End your prayer time by praising God again and committing your day to Him.

Now to him who is able to do immeasurably more than all we ask or imagine, according to his power that is at work within us, to him be glory in the church and in Christ Jesus throughout all generations, for ever and ever! Amen.

Ephesians 3:20-21

Suggested Activity: Declare your trust in God's plans and thank Him for hearing your prayers.

— A GENERAL ONE-HOUR PRAYER —

Praise (5 Minutes): Praise God for the things that are on your mind right now. Praise Him for one special thing He has done in your life in the past week. Praise Him for His goodness to your family (see Luke 1:68).

Wait (5 Minutes): Spend time waiting on the Lord. Be silent and let Him pull together reflections for you (see Psalm 27:14).

Confession (5 Minutes): Ask the Holy Spirit to show you anything in your life that might be displeasing to Him. Ask Him to point out attitudes that are wrong, as well as specific acts for which you have not yet made a prayer of confession. Now, confess that to the Lord so that you might be cleansed (see Psalm 32:5).

Read the Word (10 Minutes): Spend time reading the Psalms and passages on prayer located in the New Testament (see Colossians 1).

Pray the Word (10 Minutes): Pray specific passages relating to your concerns. Scriptural prayers, as well as a number of the psalms, lend themselves well to this purpose (see Psalm 119:1-56).

Thanksgiving (5 Minutes): Give thanks to the Lord for His goodness in your life, in your family, and in your church (see Colossians 2:6-7).

Meditate (5 Minutes): Ask the Lord to speak to you. Have a pen and paper ready to record impressions He gives you (see Joshua 1:8).

Listen (10 Minutes): Spend time merging the things you have read, things you have prayed, and things you have sung, and see how the Lord brings them all together to speak to you (see Isaiah 55:3).

Praise (5 Minutes): Praise the Lord for the time you have had to spend with Him and the impressions He has given you. Praise Him for His glorious attributes (see Ephesians 1:3-8).

— PRAYING AGAINST STRONGHOLDS —

This structure allows you to engage deeply in prayer while addressing strongholds with faith and intentionality.

Praise and Worship (10 Minutes):

The LORD is my rock, my fortress and my deliverer; my God is my rock, in whom I take refuge.

Psalm 18:2

Suggested Activity: Play worship music or sing hymns that declare God's power and victory over darkness.

Confession and Repentance (5 Minutes):

The weapons we fight with are not the weapons of the world. On the contrary, they have divine power to demolish strongholds. 2 Corinthians 10:4

Suggested Activity: Ask the Holy Spirit to show you areas of sin or weakness where strongholds may have taken root and confess them to God.

Declaring God's Authority (10 Minutes):

I have given you authority to trample on snakes and scorpions and to overcome all the power of the enemy; nothing will harm you. Luke 10:19

Suggested Activity: Speak aloud declarations of God's authority over your life and the breaking of strongholds.

Praying the Word (10 Minutes:

No weapon forged against you will prevail, and you will refute every tongue that accuses you.
Isaiah 54:17

Suggested Activity: Choose specific scriptures that address the strongholds you are battling and pray them over your life.

Intercession (10 Minutes):

Carry each other's burdens, and in this way, you will fulfill the law of Christ.　　　Galatians 6:2

Suggested Activity: Pray for others who may be struggling with strongholds, lifting them up to God for deliverance.

Binding and Loosing (10 Minutes):

Truly I tell you, whatever you bind on earth will be bound in heaven, and whatever you lose on earth will be loosed in heaven.　　　Matthew 18:18

Suggested Activity: Verbally bind the works of the enemy and loose God's blessings and freedom in your life.

Thanksgiving and Victory Declaration (5 Minutes):

But thanks be to God! He gives us the victory through our Lord Jesus Christ.　　　1 Corinthians 15:57

Suggested Activity: End your prayer time with thanksgiving for the victory God has already won and declare His promises over your life.

— PRAYING AGAINST THE SPIRIT OF NICOTINE ADDICTION —

Praise and Worship (10 Minutes)

Enter his gates with thanksgiving and his courts with praise; give thanks to him and praise his name. Psalm 100:4

Suggested Activity: Begin by praising God for His power and faithfulness, singing worship songs, or declaring His greatness aloud, inviting His presence into the prayer.

Repentance and Cleansing (10 Minutes):

If we confess our sins, he is faithful and just and will forgive us our sins and purify us from all un-righteousness. 1 John 1:9

Suggested Activity: Confess any personal or generational sins related to addiction. Ask for forgiveness and cleansing through the blood of Jesus.

Breaking Strongholds (10 Minutes):

The weapons we fight with are not the weapons of the world. On the contrary, they have divine power to demolish strongholds.   2 Corinthians 10:4

Suggested Activity: Declare freedom from the bondage of nicotine. Speak against the stronghold of addiction and proclaim the power of Christ to break every chain.

Binding and Rebuking the Spirit of Addiction (10 Minutes):

Truly I tell you, whatever you bind on earth will be bound in heaven, and whatever you loose on earth will be loosed in heaven.   Matthew 18:18

Suggested Activity: In Jesus' name, bind and rebuke the spirit of nicotine addiction. Command it to leave and declare that it has no authority over you or others.

Inviting the Holy Spirit for Healing and Restoration (10 Minutes):

Now the Lord is the Spirit; and where the Spirit of the Lord is, there is freedom.   2 Corinthians 3:17

Suggested Activity: Pray for the Holy Spirit to fill the void left by addiction. Ask for healing of the body, mind, and spirit and for strength to resist temptation.

Thanksgiving and Declaration of Victory (10 Minutes):

But thanks be to God! He gives us the victory through our Lord Jesus Christ.   1 Corinthians 15:57

Suggested Activity: Thank God for the victory over nicotine addiction. Declare freedom and dedicate your body as a temple of the Holy Spirit (see 1 Corinthians 6:19-20).

— PRAYING AGAINST TERRITORIAL SPIRITS —

To pray for an hour against territorial spirits in a region, you can divide the time into segments, each focused on a specific aspect of spiritual warfare.

Praise and Worship (10 Minutes):

Enter his gates with thanksgiving and his courts with praise; give thanks to him and praise his name. Psalm 100:4

Suggested Activity: Begin by praising God for His sovereignty and goodness. Sing worship songs or declare His attributes aloud. This invites His presence and sets the atmosphere for prayer.

Repentance and Cleansing (10 Minutes):

If we confess our sins, he is faithful and just and will forgive us our sins and purify us from all un-righteousness. 1 John 1:9

Suggested Activity: Confess any personal or collective sins that might hinder prayer. Ask for forgiveness and the cleansing power of the blood of Jesus over yourself and the region.

Declaring God's Authority Over the Region (10 Minutes):

The earth is the LORD's, and everything in it, the world, and all who live in it. Psalm 24:1

Suggested Activity: Proclaim God's ownership and authority over the region. Declare that Jesus is Lord over the land and renounce any claim the enemy might have.

Binding and Rebuking Territorial Spirits (10 Minutes):

Truly I tell you, whatever you bind on earth will be bound in heaven, and whatever you loose on earth will be loosed in heaven. Matthew 18:18

Suggested Activity: Bind and rebuke in Jesus' name any territorial spirits operating in the region. Speak against their influence and command them to leave. Plead the blood of Jesus over the land.

Inviting the Holy Spirit (10 Minutes):

Now the Lord is the Spirit; and where the Spirit of the Lord is, there is freedom. 2 Corinthians 3:17

Suggested Activity: Pray for the Holy Spirit to fill the region with His presence, bringing peace, revival, and transformation. Ask Him to empower believers in the area.

Thanksgiving and Declaration of Victory (10 Minutes):

But thanks be to God! He gives us the victory through our Lord Jesus Christ."　　1 Corinthians 15:57

Suggested Activity: End your hour of prayer with thanksgiving for the victory already won through Jesus. Declare that the region is free and dedicated to God's glory. Sing a final song of praise or speak a blessing over the land.

— PRAYING WHEN YOU FEEL ALONE —

Praying for an hour when you feel alone can be a deeply comforting and transformative experience.

Praise and Worship (10 Minutes):

But thou art holy, O thou that inhabitest the praises of Israel. Psalm 22:3, KJV

Suggested Activity: Begin by praising God for His presence and faithfulness. Sing worship songs or speak words of adoration, acknowledging His greatness and love.

Acknowledging God's Presence (10 Minutes):

Where can I go from your Spirit? Where can I flee from your presence? If I go up to the heavens, you

are there; if I make my bed in the depths, you are
there. Psalm 139:7-8

Suggested Activity: Reflect on God's omnipresence. Speak to Him as though He is right there with you because He is. Share your thoughts and feelings with Him openly.

Confession and Cleansing (10 Minutes):

If we confess our sins, he is faithful and just and will forgive us our sins and purify us from all un-righteousness. 1 John 1:9

Suggested Activity: Confess any sins or burdens weighing on your heart and ask for forgiveness and cleansing through the blood of Jesus.

Reading and Meditating on Scripture (10 Minutes):

Keep this Book of the Law always on your lips; meditate on it day and night, so that you may be careful to do everything written in it. Joshua 1:8

Suggested Activity: Read passages of scripture that bring comfort and encouragement, such as Psalm 23 or Isaiah 41:10. Meditate on their meaning and how they apply to your life.

Petition and Intercession (10 Minutes):

Do not be anxious about anything, but in every situation, by prayer and petition, with thanksgiving, present your requests to God.

Philippians 4:6

Suggested Activity: Present your personal needs and concerns to God. Then, intercede for others who may be struggling or feeling alone.

Thanksgiving (10 Minutes):

Give thanks in all circumstances; for this is God's will for you in Christ Jesus.   1 Thessalonians 5:18

Suggested Activity: Thank God for His blessings, even in the midst of loneliness. Express thanksgiving for His love, provision, and the hope He gives.

Listening and Reflection:

Whether you turn to the right or to the left, your ears will hear a voice behind you, saying, "This is the way; walk in it."   Isaiah 30:21

Suggested Activity: Spend time in silence, listening for God's voice. Reflect on what He may be speaking to your heart and write down any impressions or thoughts you receive.

— WAGING SPIRITUAL WARFARE IN PRAYER —

Waging spiritual warfare for an hour can be a powerful and structured way to engage in prayer.

Praise and Worship (10 Minutes): Begin by praising God for His greatness and faithfulness. Worship sets the tone for spiritual warfare.

Enter His gates with thanksgiving and His courts with praise; give thanks to him and praise his name. Psalm 100:4

Suggested Activity: Reflect on specific things you're grateful for and express your thanks.

Confession and Repentance (5 Minutes): Confess your sins and ask for forgiveness. This ensures your heart is clean before God.

If we confess our sins, He is faithful and just to forgive us our sins and to cleanse us from all unrighteousness.　　　　　1 John 1:9, NKJV

Suggested Activity: Spend time in silent prayer, asking the Holy Spirit to reveal areas where you need repentance.

Pray for the Armor of God (10 Minutes): Pray through the armor of God, asking Him for spiritual protection and strength.

Put on the full armor of God, so that you can take your stand against the devil's schemes.
　　　　　Ephesians 6:11

Suggested Activity: Visualize putting on each piece of armor (e.g., the helmet of salvation, the shield of faith) while praying through Ephesians 6:10-18.

Binding and Loosing (10 Minutes): Declare authority over the enemy, binding his works and loosing God's blessings.

Whatever you bind on earth will be bound in heaven, and whatever you loose on earth will be loosed in heaven.　　　　Matthew 18:18, NKJV

Suggested Activity: Declare aloud what you are binding (e.g., fear, doubt) and what you are losing (e.g., peace, joy).

Praying the Word (10 Minutes): Use specific scriptures to declare victory over spiritual battles.

No weapon formed against you shall prosper.
　　　　　　　　　Isaiah 54:17, NKJV

Suggested Activity: Choose specific scriptures related to your situation, write them down, and read them aloud as declarations.

Intercession (10 Minutes): Pray for others, including family, friends, and those in need of spiritual breakthrough.

I urge, then, first of all, that petitions, prayers, intercession and thanksgiving be made for all people.

1 Timothy 2:1

Suggested Activity: Make a list of people or situations to pray for and spend time lifting each one up in prayer before the Lord.

Thanksgiving and Declaration (5 Minutes): End your hour of prayer with thanksgiving and declare God's promises over your life.

Give thanks in all circumstances; for this is God's will for you in Christ Jesus.   1 Thessalonians 5:1

Suggested Activity: Make a list of things you're thankful for and end by declaring God's promises over your life.

— PRAYING WHEN YOU ARE EMOTIONALLY EXHAUSTED —

Praise (5 Minutes): Start your prayer hour by praising the Lord. Praise Him for His comfort and peace in times of emotional turmoil (see Psalm 59:16 and Ephesians 1:3-8).

Wait (5 Minutes): Spend time waiting on the Lord. Be silent and let Him soothe your troubled heart (see Psalm 46:10).

Confession (5 Minutes): Ask the Holy Spirit to show you any emotional burdens you need to release. Confess your feelings of exhaustion and ask for His healing (see Psalm 51:17).

Read the Word (5 Minutes): Spend time reading passages that speak of God's comfort and healing (see Matthew 11:28-30).

Petition (5 Minutes): Make specific requests on behalf of yourself for emotional healing and peace (see Philippians 4:6-7).

Intercession (5 Minutes): Make requests on behalf of others who may also be experiencing emotional exhaustion (see James 5:16).

Pray the Word (5 Minutes): Pray specific passages that speak of God's comfort and peace (see Romans 8:26).

Thanksgiving (5 Minutes): Give thanks to the Lord for His promise of comfort and healing (see Colossians 3:15).

Singing (5 Minutes): Sing songs of praise or worship that focus on God's comfort and peace (see Psalm 59:16).

Meditate (5 Minutes): Ask the Lord to speak to you and bring peace to your heart. Have a pen and paper ready to record impressions He gives you (see Joshua 1:8).

Listen (5 Minutes): Spend time merging the things you have read, things you have prayed, and things you have sung, and see how the Lord brings them all together to speak to you (see Isaiah 55:3).

Praise (5 Minutes): Praise the Lord for the time you have had to spend with Him and the comfort He has given you. Praise Him for His glorious attributes (see Ephesians 1:3-8).

— PRAYING WHEN YOU ARE EXPERIENCING ANXIETY —

Praise (5 Minutes): Praise God for His peace and comfort in times of anxiety (see Psalm 107:9).

Wait (5 Minutes): Spend time waiting on the Lord. Be silent and let Him calm your anxious thoughts (see Psalm 46:10).

Confession (5 Minutes): Ask the Holy Spirit to show you any anxious thoughts you need to release. Confess your anxiety and ask for His peace (see Philippians 4:6-7).

Read the Word (5 Minutes): Spend time reading passages that speak of God's peace and comfort (see Matthew 11:28-30).

Petition (5 Minutes): Make specific requests on behalf of yourself for peace and relief from anxiety (see 1 Peter 5:7).

Intercession (5 Minutes): Make requests on behalf of others who may also be experiencing anxiety (see James 5:16).

Pray the Word (5 Minutes): Pray specific passages that speak of God's peace and comfort (see Philippians 4:6-7).

Thanksgiving (5 Minutes): Give thanks to the Lord for His promise of peace and comfort (see Colossians 3:15).

Singing (5 Minutes): Sing songs of praise or worship that focus on God's peace and comfort (see Psalm 59:16).

Meditate (5 Minutes): Ask the Lord to speak to you and bring peace to your heart. Have a pen and paper ready to record impressions He gives you (see Joshua 1:8).

Listen (5 Minutes): Spend time merging the things you have read, things you have prayed, and things you have sung, and see how the Lord brings them all together to speak to you (see Isaiah 55:3).

Praise (5 Minutes): Praise the Lord for the time you have had to spend with Him and the peace He has given you. Praise Him for His glorious attributes (see Ephesians 1:3-8).

— PRAYING WHEN YOU ARE EXPERIENCING STRESS —

Praise (5 Minutes): Praise God for His peace and comfort in times of stress (see 2 Corinthians 1:3-4).

Wait (5 Minutes): Spend time waiting on the Lord. Be silent and let Him calm your stressed thoughts (see Psalm 55:18).

Confession (5 Minutes): Ask the Holy Spirit to show you any stressful thoughts you need to release. Confess your stress and ask for His peace (see Philippians 4:6-7).

Read the Word (5 Minutes): Spend time reading passages that speak of God's peace and comfort (see Matthew 11:28-30).

Petition (5 Minutes): Make specific requests on behalf of yourself for peace and relief from stress (see 1 Peter 5:7).

Intercession (5 Minutes): Make requests on behalf of others who may also be experiencing stress (see James 5:16).

Pray the Word (5 Minutes): Pray specific passages that speak of God's peace and comfort (see Philippians 4:7).

Thanksgiving (5 Minutes): Give thanks to the Lord for His promise of peace and comfort (seen Colossians 3:15).

Singing (5 Minutes): Sing songs of praise or worship that focus on God's peace and comfort (see Psalm 59:16).

Meditate (5 Minutes): Ask the Lord to speak to you and bring peace to your heart. Have a pen and paper ready to record impressions He gives you (see Joshua 1:8).

Listen (5 Minutes): Spend time merging the things you have read, things you have prayed, and things you have sung, and see how the Lord brings them all together to speak to you (see Isaiah 55:3).

Praise (5 Minutes): Praise the Lord for the time you have had to spend with Him and the peace He has given you. Praise Him for His glorious attributes (see Isaiah 25:1).

— PRAYING WHEN YOU ARE EXPERIENCING DEPRESSION —

Praise (5 Minutes): Praise God for His comfort and peace in times of depression (see Psalm 34:18).

Wait (5 Minutes): Spend time waiting on the Lord. Be silent and let Him soothe your troubled heart (see Psalm 46:10).

Confession (5 Minutes): Ask the Holy Spirit to show you any emotional burdens you need to release. Confess your feelings of depression and ask for His healing (see Psalm 51:17).

Read the Word (5 Minutes): Spend time reading passages that speak of God's comfort and healing (see Matthew 11:28-30).

Pray the Word (5 Minutes): Pray specific passages that speak of God's comfort and peace (see Psalm 23).

Petition (5 Minutes): Make specific requests on behalf of yourself for emotional healing and peace (see Philippians 4:6-7).

Intercession (5 Minutes): Make requests on behalf of others who may also be experiencing depression (see James 5:16).

Thanksgiving (5 Minutes): Give thanks to the Lord for His promise of comfort and healing (see Colossians 3:15).

Singing (5 Minutes): Sing songs of praise or worship that focus on God's comfort and peace (see Psalm 59:16).

Meditate (5 Minutes): Ask the Lord to speak to you and bring peace to your heart. Have a pen and paper ready to record impressions He gives you (see Joshua 1:8).

Listen (5 Minutes): Spend time merging the things you have read, things you have prayed, and things you have sung, and see how the Lord brings them all together to speak to you (see Isaiah 55:3).

Praise (5 Minutes): Praise the Lord for the time you have had to spend with Him and the comfort He has given you. Praise Him for His glorious attributes (see Ephesians 1:3-8).

— PRAYING WHEN YOU ARE EXPERIENCING GRIEF —

Praise (5 Minutes): Praise God for His comfort and peace in times of grief (see Psalm 34:18).

Confession (5 Minutes): Ask the Holy Spirit to show you any emotional burdens you need to release. Confess your feelings of grief and ask for His healing (see Psalm 51:17).

Read the Word (10 Minutes): Spend time reading passages that speak of God's comfort and healing (see Ecclesiastes 3:1-17).

Petition (5 Minutes): Make specific requests on behalf of yourself for emotional healing and peace (see Philippians 4:6-7).

Intercession (5 Minutes): Make requests on behalf of others who may also be experiencing grief (see James 5:16).

Pray the Word (10 Minutes): Pray specific passages that speak of God's comfort and peace (see Psalm 23).

Thanksgiving (5 Minutes): Give thanks to the Lord for His promise of comfort and healing (see Colossians 3:15).

Meditate (5 Minutes): Ask the Lord to speak to you and bring peace to your heart. Have a pen and paper ready to record impressions He gives you (see Joshua 1:8).

Listen (5 Minutes): Spend time merging the things you have read, things you have prayed, and things you have sung, and see how the Lord brings them all together to speak to you (see Isaiah 55:3).

Praise (5 Minutes): Praise the Lord for the time you have had to spend with Him and the comfort He has given you. Praise Him for His glorious attributes (see Ephesians 1:3-8).

— PRAYING WHEN YOU ARE EXPERIENCING LONELINESS —

Praise (5 Minutes): Praise God for His presence and for being with you even in times of loneliness (see Psalm 23:4).

Wait (5 Minutes): Spend time waiting on the Lord. Be silent and let Him fill your heart with His presence (see Psalm 46:10).

Confession (5 Minutes): Ask the Holy Spirit to show you any feelings of loneliness you need to release. Confess your loneliness and ask for His comfort (see Psalm 34:18).

Read the Word (5 Minutes): Spend time reading passages that speak of God's presence and comfort (see Romans 8:35-39).

Petition (5 Minutes): Make specific requests on behalf of yourself for comfort and relief from loneliness (see Philippians 4:6-7).

Intercession (5 Minutes): Make requests on behalf of others who may also be experiencing loneliness (see James 5:16).

Pray the Word (5 Minutes): Pray specific passages that speak of God's presence and comfort (see Psalm 23).

Thanksgiving (5 Minutes): Give thanks to the Lord for His promise of comfort and His presence (see Colossians 3:15).

Singing (5 Minutes): Sing songs of praise or worship that focus on God's presence and comfort (see Psalm 9:16).

Meditate (5 Minutes): Ask the Lord to speak to you and bring comfort to your heart. Have a pen and paper ready to record impressions He gives you (see Joshua 1:8).

Listen (5 Minutes): Spend time merging the things you have read, things you have prayed, and things you have sung, and see how the Lord brings them all together to speak to you (see Isaiah 55:3).

Praise (5 Minutes): Praise the Lord for the time you have had to spend with Him and the comfort He has given you. Praise Him for His glorious attributes (see Ephesians 1:3-8).

— PRAYING WHEN YOU ARE EXPERIENCING FEAR —

Praise (5 Minutes): Praise God for His protection and for being your Refuge in times of fear (see Psalm 27:1).

Wait (5 Minutes): Spend time waiting on the Lord. Be silent and let Him calm your fearful thoughts (see Lamentations 3:25).

Confession (5 Minutes): Ask the Holy Spirit to show you any fearful thoughts you need to release. Confess your fear and ask for His peace (see Philippians 4:6-7).

Read the Word (5 Minutes): Spend time reading passages that speak of God's protection and peace (see Isaiah 41:10).

Petition (5 Minutes): Make specific requests on behalf of yourself for peace and relief from fear (see 1 Peter 5:7).

Intercession (5 Minutes): Make requests on behalf of others who may also be experiencing fear (see James 5:16).

Pray the Word (5 Minutes): Pray specific passages that speak of God's protection and peace (see Psalm 23).

Thanksgiving (5 Minutes): Give thanks to the Lord for His promise of protection and peace (see Colossians 3:15).

Singing (5 Minutes): Sing songs of praise or worship that focus on God's protection and peace (see Psalm 59:16).

Meditate (5 Minutes): Ask the Lord to speak to you and bring peace to your heart. Have a pen and paper ready to record impressions He gives you (see Joshua 1:8).

Listen (5 Minutes): Spend time merging the things you have read, things you have prayed, and things you have sung, and see how the Lord brings them all together to speak to you (see Isaiah 55:3).

Praise (5 Minutes): Praise the Lord for the time you have had to spend with Him and the peace He has given you. Praise Him for His glorious attributes (see Ephesians 1:3-8).

— PRAYING WHEN YOU ARE EXPERIENCING ANGER —

Praise (5 Minutes): Praise God for His peace and comfort in times of anger (see Psalm 34:4).

Wait (5 Minutes): Spend time waiting on the Lord. Be silent and let Him calm your angry thoughts (see Psalm 46:10).

Confession (5 Minutes): Ask the Holy Spirit to show you any angry thoughts you need to release. Confess your anger and ask for His peace (see Philippians 4:6-7).

Read the Word (5 Minutes): Spend time reading passages that speak of God's peace and comfort (see Matthew 11:28-30).

Petition (5 Minutes): Make specific requests on behalf of yourself for peace and relief from anger (see 1 Peter 5:7).

Intercession (5 Minutes): Make requests on behalf of others who may also be experiencing anger (see James 5:16).

Pray the Word (5 Minutes): Pray specific passages that speak of God's peace and comfort (see Psalm 23).

Thanksgiving (5 Minutes): Give thanks to the Lord for His promise of peace and comfort (see Colossians 3:15).

Singing (5 Minutes): Sing songs of praise or worship that focus on God's peace and comfort (see Psalm 59:16).

Meditate (5 Minutes): Ask the Lord to speak to you and bring peace to your heart. Have a pen and paper ready to record impressions He gives you (see Joshua 1:8).

Listen (5 Minutes): Spend time merging the things you have read, things you have prayed, and things you have sung, and see how the Lord brings them all together to speak to you (see Isaiah 55:3).

Praise (5 Minutes): Praise the Lord for the time you have had to spend with Him and the peace He has given you. Praise Him for His glorious attributes (see Ephesians 1:3-8).

— PRAYING, FOCUSING ON FORGIVENESS —

Praise (5 Minutes): Start your prayer hour by praising the Lord. Praise Him for His mercy and grace in forgiving our sins (see Psalm 103:1-3).

Wait (5 Minutes): Spend time waiting on the Lord. Be silent and let Him bring to mind areas where you need forgiveness (see Isaiah 40:31).

Confession (5 Minutes): Ask the Holy Spirit to show you any sins you need to confess. Confess your sins and ask for God's forgiveness (see 1 John 1:9).

Read the Word (5 Minutes): Spend time reading passages that speak of God's forgiveness and mercy (see Ephesians 1:7).

Petition (5 Minutes): Make specific requests on behalf of yourself for forgiveness and a clean heart (see Psalm 51:10).

Intercession (5 Minutes): Make requests on behalf of others who may also need forgiveness (see James 5:16).

Pray the Word (5 Minutes): Pray specific passages that speak of God's forgiveness and mercy (see Psalm 32:1-2).

Thanksgiving (5 Minutes): Give thanks to the Lord for His promise of forgiveness and mercy (see Colossians 3:13).

Singing (5 Minutes): Sing songs of praise or worship that focus on God's forgiveness and mercy (see Psalm 103:12).

Meditate (5 Minutes): Ask the Lord to speak to you and bring peace to your heart. Have a pen and paper ready to record impressions He gives you (see Joshua 1:8).

Listen (5 Minutes): Spend time merging the things you have read, things you have prayed, and things you have sung, and see how the Lord brings them all together to speak to you (see Isaiah 55:3).

Praise (5 Minutes): Praise the Lord for the time you have had to spend with Him and the forgiveness He has given you. Praise Him for His glorious attributes (see Ephesians 1:3-8).

— PRAYING, FOCUSING ON HOPE —

Praise (5 Minutes): Start your prayer hour by praising the Lord. Praise Him for being the Source of our hope and for His promises that give us hope (see Psalm 71:5).

Wait (5 Minutes): Spend time waiting on the Lord. Be silent and let Him fill your heart with hope (Micah 7:7).

Confession (5 Minutes): Ask the Holy Spirit to show you any areas where you have lost hope. Confess your doubts and ask for His renewal of hope (see Romans 15:13).

Read the Word (5 Minutes): Spend time reading passages that speak of God's hope and promises (see Jeremiah 29:11).

Petition (5 Minutes): Make specific requests on behalf of yourself for hope and encouragement (see Psalm 33:22).

Intercession (5 Minutes): Make requests on behalf of others who may also need hope (see Romans 12:12).

Pray the Word (5 Minutes): Pray specific passages that speak of God's hope and promises (see Psalm 130:5).

Thanksgiving (5 Minutes): Give thanks to the Lord for His promise of hope and for the hope He has given you (see Colossians 1:27).

Meditate (5 Minutes): Ask the Lord to speak to you and fill your heart with hope. Have a pen and paper ready to record impressions He gives you (see Joshua 1:8).

Listen (10 Minutes): Spend time merging the things you have read, things you have prayed, and things you have sung, and see how the Lord brings them all together to speak to you (see Isaiah 55:3).

Praise (5 Minutes): Praise the Lord for the time you have had to spend with Him and the hope He has given you. Praise Him for His glorious attributes (see Ephesians 1:3-8).

— PRAYING, FOCUSING ON HEALING —

Praise (5 Minutes): Start your prayer hour by praising the Lord. Praise Him for His healing power and for being the Source of all healing (see Psalm 103:2-3).

Wait (5 Minutes): Spend time waiting on the Lord. Be silent and let Him fill your heart with His healing presence (see Isaiah 40:31).

Confession (5 Minutes): Ask the Holy Spirit to show you any areas where you need healing. Confess your need for healing and ask for His healing touch (see James 5:16).

Read the Word (5 Minutes): Spend time reading passages that speak of God's healing promises (see Jeremiah 17:14).

Petition (5 Minutes): Make specific requests on behalf of yourself for physical, emotional, or spiritual healing (see Psalm 30:2).

Intercession (5 Minutes): Make requests on behalf of others who may also need healing (see Isaiah 53:5).

Pray the Word (10 Minutes): Pray specific passages that speak of God's healing promises (see Psalm 107:20).

Thanksgiving (5 Minutes): Give thanks to the Lord for His promise of healing and for the healing He has given you (see Colossians 3:15).

Meditate (5 Minutes): Ask the Lord to speak to you and fill your heart with His healing presence. Have a pen and paper ready to record impressions He gives you (see Joshua 1:8).

Listen (10 Minutes): Spend time merging the things you have read, things you have prayed and things you have sung, and see how the Lord brings them all together to speak to you (see Isaiah 55:3).

— PRAYING FOR WISDOM —

Praise (5 Minutes): Praise God for His wisdom and for being the Source of all understanding (see Proverbs 2:6).

Wait (5 Minutes): Spend time waiting on the Lord. Be silent and let Him fill your heart with His wisdom (see Psalm 27:13-14).

Confession (5 Minutes): Ask the Holy Spirit to show you any areas where you need wisdom. Confess your need for wisdom and ask for His guidance (see James 1:5).

Read the Word (5 Minutes): Spend time reading passages that speak of God's wisdom and promises (see Proverbs 3:5-6).

Petition (5 Minutes): Make specific requests on behalf of yourself for wisdom and understanding (see Colossians 1:9).

Pray the Word (10 Minutes): Pray specific passages that speak of God's wisdom and promises (see Psalm 119:105).

Thanksgiving (5 Minutes): Give thanks to the Lord for His promise of wisdom and for the wisdom He has given you (see Colossians 3:16).

Meditate (5 Minutes): Ask the Lord to speak to you and fill your heart with His wisdom. Have a pen and paper ready to record impressions He gives you (see Joshua 1:8).

Listen (10 Minutes): Spend time merging the things you have read, things you have prayed, and things you have sung, and see how the Lord brings them all together to speak to you (see Isaiah 55:3).

Praise (5 Minutes): Praise the Lord for the time you have had to spend with Him and the wisdom He has given you. Praise Him for His glorious attributes (see Ephesians 1:3-8).

— PRAYING, FOCUSING ON PEACE —

Praise (5 Minutes): Praise God for His peace and comfort in times of turmoil (see Psalm 34:4).

Wait (5 Minutes): Spend time waiting on the Lord. Be silent and let Him calm your anxious thoughts (see Psalm 37:7).

Confession (5 Minutes): Ask the Holy Spirit to show you any anxious thoughts you need to release. Confess your anxiety and ask for His peace (see Philippians 4:6-7).

Read the Word (5 Minutes): Spend time reading passages that speak of God's peace and comfort (see Matthew 11:28-30).

Petition (5 Minutes): Make specific requests on behalf of yourself for peace and relief from anxiety (see 1 Peter 5:7).

Intercession (5 Minutes): Make requests on behalf of others who may also be experiencing anxiety (see James 5:16).

Pray the Word (5 Minutes): Pray specific passages that speak of God's peace and comfort (see Psalm 23).

Thanksgiving (5 Minutes): Give thanks to the Lord for His promise of peace and comfort (see Colossians 3:15).

Singing (5 Minutes): Sing songs of praise or worship that focus on God's peace and comfort (see Psalm 59:16).

Meditate (5 Minutes): Ask the Lord to speak to you and bring peace to your heart. Have a pen and paper ready to record impressions He gives you (see Joshua 1:8).

Listen (5 Minutes): Spend time merging the things you have read, things you have prayed, and things you have sung, and see how the Lord brings them all together to speak to you (see Isaiah 55:3).

Praise (5 Minutes): Praise the Lord for the time you have had to spend with Him and the peace He has given you. Praise Him for His glorious attributes (see Ephesians 1:3-8).

— PRAYING, FOCUSING ON STRENGTH —

Praise (5 Minutes): Praise God for His strength and for being your Refuge in times of weariness (see Psalm 28:7).

Wait (5 Minutes): Spend time waiting on the Lord. Be silent and let Him renew your strength (see Isaiah 40:31).

Confession (5 Minutes): Ask the Holy Spirit to show you anything in your life that might be displeasing to Him. Confess your fatigue and ask for His cleansing and renewal (see Psalm 51:10).

Read the Word (5 Minutes): Spend time reading passages that speak of God's strength and renewal (see Matthew 11:28-30).

Petition (5 Minutes): Make specific requests on behalf of yourself for physical strength and renewal (see Philippians 4:13).

Intercession (5 Minutes): Make requests on behalf of others who may also be experiencing physical tiredness (see James 5:16).

Pray the Word (5 Minutes): Pray specific passages that speak of God's strength and renewal (see Psalm 23).

Thanksgiving (5 Minutes): Give thanks to the Lord for His promise of rest and renewal (see Colossians 3:15).

Singing (5 Minutes): Sing songs of praise or worship that focus on God's strength and renewal (see Psalm 59:16).

Meditate (5 Minutes): Ask the Lord to speak to you and renew your strength. Have a pen and paper ready to record impressions He gives you (see Joshua 1:8).

Listen (10 Minutes): Spend time merging the things you have read, things you have prayed, and things you have sung, and see how the Lord brings them all together to speak to you (see Isaiah 55:3).

— PRAYING, FOCUSING ON HUMILITY —

Praise (5 Minutes): Start your prayer hour by praising the Lord. Praise Him for His greatness and for being the Source of all humility (see Psalm 95:6).

Wait (5 Minutes): Spend time waiting on the Lord. Be silent and let Him fill your heart with humility (see Psalm 62:5).

Confession (5 Minutes): Ask the Holy Spirit to show you any areas where you need humility. Confess your pride and ask for His guidance (see James 4:10).

Read the Word (5 Minutes): Spend time reading passages that speak of God's humility and promises (see Philippians 2:3-4).

Petition (5 Minutes): Make specific requests on behalf of yourself for humility and understanding (see Colossians 3:12).

Intercession (5 Minutes): Make requests on behalf of others who may also need humility (see Ephesians 4:2).

Pray the Word (5 Minutes): Pray specific passages that speak of God's humility and promises (see Micah 6:8).

Thanksgiving (5 Minutes): Give thanks to the Lord for His promise of humility and for the humility He has given you (see Colossians 3:15).

Singing (5 Minutes): Sing songs of praise or worship that focus on God's humility and promises (see Psalm 25:9).

Meditate (5 Minutes): Ask the Lord to speak to you and fill your heart with humility. Have a pen and paper ready to record impressions He gives you (see Joshua 1:8)

Listen (5 Minutes): Spend time merging the things you have read, things you have prayed, and things you have sung, and see how the Lord brings them all together to speak to you (see Isaiah 55:3).

Praise (5 Minutes): Praise the Lord for the time you have had to spend with Him and the humility He has given you. Praise Him for His glorious attributes (see Ephesians 1:3-8).

— PRAYING, FOCUSING ON LOVE —

Praise (5 Minutes): Praise God for His love and for being the Source of all love (see 1 John 4:8).

Wait (5 Minutes): Spend time waiting on the Lord. Be silent and let Him fill your heart with His love (see Psalm 37:7).

Confession (5 Minutes): Ask the Holy Spirit to show you any areas where you need to grow in love. Confess your shortcomings and ask for His guidance (see 1 Corinthians 13:4-7).

Read the Word (5 Minutes): Spend time reading passages that speak of God's love and promises (see John 3:16).

Petition (5 Minutes): Make specific requests on behalf of yourself for love and understanding (see Colossians 3:14).

Intercession (5 Minutes): Make requests on behalf of others who may also need love (see Ephesians 3:17-19).

Pray the Word (5 Minutes): Pray specific passages that speak of God's love and promises (see Romans 8:38-39).

Thanksgiving (5 Minutes): Give thanks to the Lord for His promise of love and for the love He has given you (see Colossians 3:15).

Singing (5 Minutes): Sing songs of praise or worship that focus on God's love and promises (see Psalm 136:1).

Meditate (5 Minutes): Ask the Lord to speak to you and fill your heart with His love. Have a pen and paper ready to record impressions He gives you (see Joshua 1:8).

Listen (5 Minutes): Spend time merging the things you have read, things you have prayed, and things you have sung, and see how the Lord brings them all together to speak to you (see Isaiah 55:3).

Praise (5 Minutes): Praise the Lord for the time you have had to spend with Him and the love He has given you. Praise Him for His glorious attributes (see Ephesians 1:3-8).

— PRAYING, FOCUSING ON BLENDED FAMILIES —

Praise (5 Minutes): Praise God for His love and for bringing your blended family together (see Psalm 133:1).

Wait (5 Minutes): Spend time waiting on the Lord. Be silent and let Him fill your heart with His presence (see 2 Peter 3:9).

Confession (5 Minutes): Ask the Holy Spirit to show you any areas where you need to grow in love and understanding within your blended family. Confess any shortcomings and ask for His guidance (see Colossians 3:13).

Read the Word (5 Minutes): Spend time reading passages that speak of God's love, unity, and promises for families (see Ephesians 4:2-3).

Petition (5 Minutes): Make specific requests on behalf of yourself and your blended family for love, patience, and unity (Philippians 2:2).

Intercession (5 Minutes): Make requests on behalf of other blended families who may also need love and understanding (see Romans 12:10). Rebuke role confusion, where stepparents, biological parents, and children struggle to understand their positions in the new family dynamic. Speak adjustment to new family dynamics and loose adaptation to a new parental figure. Pray that all concerned adapt to new routines, rules, and communication styles. Declare the blood of Jesus to resolve emotions as each one adjusts to the reality of their new family.

Pray the Word (5 Minutes): Pray specific passages that speak of God's love and unity for families (see Psalm 133:1).

Thanksgiving (5 Minutes): Give thanks to the Lord for His promise of love and unity and for the blessings He has given your blended family (see Colossians 3:15).

Singing (5 Minutes): Sing songs of praise or worship that focus on God's love and unity (see Psalm 136:1).

Meditate (5 Minutes): Ask the Lord to speak to you and fill your heart with His love and understanding. Have a pen and paper ready to record impressions He gives you (see Joshua 1:8).

Listen (5 Minutes): Spend time merging the things you have read, things you have prayed, and things you have sung, and see how the Lord brings them all together to speak to you (see Isaiah 55:3).

Praise (5 Minutes): Praise the Lord for the time you have had to spend with Him and the love and unity He has given your blended family. Praise Him for His glorious attributes (see Ephesians 1:3-8).

— PRAYING FOR SUPERNATURAL FAVOR —

Praise (5 Minutes): Praise God for His favor and for being the Source of all blessings (see Psalm 5:12).

Wait (5 Minutes): Spend time waiting on the Lord. Be silent and let Him fill your heart with His favor (see Psalm 33:20-22).

Confession (5 Minutes): Ask the Holy Spirit to show you any areas where you need favor. Confess your need for favor and ask for His guidance (see Psalm 32:5).

Read the Word (5 Minutes): Spend time reading passages that speak of God's favor and promises (see Psalm 84:11).

Petition (5 Minutes): Make specific requests on behalf of yourself for supernatural favor and blessings (see Proverbs 3:4).

Intercession (5 Minutes): Make requests on behalf of others who may also need favor (see 1 Timothy 2:1).

Pray the Word (5 Minutes): Pray specific passages that speak of God's favor and promises (see Psalm 23).

Thanksgiving (5 Minutes): Give thanks to the Lord for His promise of favor and for the favor He has given you (see Colossians 3:15).

Singing (5 Minutes): Sing songs of praise or worship that focus on God's favor and promises (see Psalm 59:16).

Meditate (5 Minutes): Ask the Lord to speak to you and fill your heart with His favor. Have a pen and paper ready to record impressions He gives you (see Joshua 1:8).

Listen (5 Minutes): Spend time merging the things you have read, things you have prayed, and things you have sung, and see how the Lord brings them all together to speak to you (see Isaiah 55:3).

Praise (5 Minutes): Praise the Lord for the time you have had to spend with Him and the favor He has given you. Praise Him for His glorious attributes (see Ephesians 1:3-8).

— PRAYING FOR SAFETY —

Praise (5 Minutes): Start your prayer hour by praising the Lord. Praise Him for His protection and for being your Refuge in times of danger (see Psalm 91:2).

Wait (5 Minutes): Spend time waiting on the Lord. Be silent and let Him fill your heart with His peace and protection (see Psalm 130:5).

Confession (5 Minutes): Ask the Holy Spirit to show you any areas where you need protection. Confess your fears and ask for His safeguarding (see Psalm 32:5).

Read the Word (5 Minutes): Spend time reading passages that speak of God's protection and promises (see Psalm 91).

Petition (5 Minutes): Make specific requests on behalf of yourself for safety and protection (see 2 Thessalonians 3:3).

Intercession (5 Minutes): Make requests on behalf of others who may also need protection (see 1 Timothy 2:1).

Pray the Word (5 Minutes): Pray specific passages that speak of God's protection and promises (see Psalm 121:7-8).

Thanksgiving (5 Minutes): Give thanks to the Lord for His promise of protection and for the safety He has given you (see Colossians 3:15).

Singing (5 Minutes): Sing songs of praise or worship that focus on God's protection and promises (see Psalm 59:16).

Meditate (5 Minutes): Ask the Lord to speak to you and fill your heart with His peace and protection. Have a pen and paper ready to record impressions He gives you (see Joshua 1:8).

Listen (5 Minutes): Spend time merging the things you have read, things you have prayed, and things you have sung, and see how the Lord brings them all together to speak to you (see Isaiah 55:3).

Praise (5 Minutes): Praise the Lord for the time you have had to spend with Him and the protection He has given you. Praise Him for His glorious attributes (see Ephesians 1:3-8).

— PRAYING TO BREAK SOUL TIES —

Crafting a prayer to break soul ties is a meaningful way to focus on healing and seeking spiritual clarity.

Preparation (5 Minutes): Start by creating a quiet and reflective space. Invite the Holy Spirit by playing calming music or sitting in silence. Begin with a deep breath, centering yourself.

Invocation (5 Minutes): Ask for divine guidance and protection during this prayer:

Heavenly Father, I come before You with an open heart seeking Your strength and wisdom. I ask You, Holy Spirit, to guide me and for Your protection during this time of reflection and renewal.

Confession (10 Minutes): Confess the soul ties you wish to address. This could be with a person, situation, or even a past experience. Acknowledge what this connection has brought into your life—both positive and negative. Express appreciation for lessons learned and a desire to release any unhealthy ties.

Release and Forgiveness (20 Minutes): Pray for the release of these ties, seeking healing and restoration:

Lord, I release this bond into Your hands, trusting You to sever any ties that no longer serve my well-being or Your purpose for my life. I forgive myself and others involved, and I ask for Your forgiveness where I've failed. Let Your love restore my soul.

Suggested Activity: Spend some time in silence, meditating on letting go.

Renewal and Blessing (15 Minutes): Invite divine love and peace to fill the spaces where the ties once existed:

Fill me with Your love and renew my spirit, Lord. I pray for blessings upon those connected to these ties and ask for Your guidance as I move forward, free and whole.

Closing (5 Minutes): End your prayer with thanksgiving and trust:

Thank You, Lord, for hearing my prayer. I trust in Your power and grace. Amen!

Suggested Activity: Take a moment to breathe deeply, feeling the peace within.

— PRAYING AGAINST FRUSTRATION —

Preparation (5 Minutes): Start by creating a quiet and reflective space. Play calming music or sit in silence.

Invocation (5 Minutes): Ask for divine guidance and protection during this prayer:

Heavenly Father, in Jesus' name I come before You with an open heart, seeking Your strength and wisdom. I ask You, Holy Spirit, to guide me and for Your protection during this time of reflection and renewal.

Acknowledgment (5 Minutes): Speak about the frustration you are experiencing, acknowledge the impact it has had on your life and express your desire to release its hold. Reflect on the importance of seeking peace and understanding.

Scripture Reading (10 Minutes): Read and meditate on scriptures that speak of God's peace and promises:

Do not be anxious about anything, but in every situation, by prayer and petition, with thanksgiving, present your requests to God. And the peace of God, which transcends all understanding, will guard your hearts and your minds in Christ Jesus.   Philippians 4:6-7

You will keep in perfect peace those whose minds are steadfast, because they trust in you.   Isaiah 26:3

Release and Forgiveness (10 Minutes): Pray for the release of frustration and seek healing and restoration:

Lord, I release this frustration into Your hands, trusting You to nullify its impact on my life. I forgive myself and others involved, and I ask for Your forgiveness where I've failed. Let Your peace restore my soul.

Now, spend some time in silence, meditating on letting go.

Renewal and Blessing (10 Minutes): Invite divine love and peace to fill the spaces where frustration once existed:

Fill me with Your love and renew my spirit, Lord. I pray for blessings upon those who have caused me frustration and ask for Your guidance as I move forward, free and whole.

Declaration of God's Peace (10 Minutes): Speak aloud declarations of God's peace over your life:

I declare that I am filled with the peace of God that transcends all understanding (see Philippians 4:7). *I trust in God's perfect plan for my life* (see Jeremiah 29:11). *I am steadfast and secure in His love* (see Isaiah 26:3).

Closing (5 Minutes): End your prayer with thanksgiving and trust:

Thank You, Lord, for hearing my prayer. I trust in Your power and grace. Amen!

Now, take a moment to breathe deeply, feeling the peace within.

— PRAYING AGAINST TEMPTATION —

Preparation (5 Minutes): Start by creating a quiet and reflective space by play calming music or sitting in silence.

Invocation (5 Minutes): Ask for divine guidance and protection during this prayer:

Heavenly Father, in Jesus' name I come before You with an open heart, seeking Your strength and wisdom. I ask You, Holy Spirit, to guide me and for Your protection during this time of reflection and renewal.

Acknowledgment (10 Minutes): Speak about the temptations you are facing. Acknowledge the impact they have had on your life and express your desire to overcome them. Reflect on the importance of seeking strength and understanding.

Scripture Reading (10 Minutes): Read and meditate on scriptures that speak of God's strength and promises:

No temptation has overtaken you except what is common to mankind. And God is faithful; he will not let you be tempted beyond what you can bear. But when you are tempted, he will also provide a way out so that you can endure it.

1 Corinthians 10:13

Blessed is the one who perseveres under trial because, having stood the test, that person will receive the crown of life that the Lord has promised to those who love him. James 1:12

Release and Forgiveness (5 Minutes): Pray for the release of these temptations and seek healing and restoration:

Lord, I release these temptations into Your hands, trusting You to nullify their impact on my life. I forgive myself and others involved, and I ask for Your forgiveness where I've faltered. Let Your strength restore my soul.

Now, spend some time in silence, meditating on letting go.

Renewal and Blessing (10 Minutes): Invite divine love and peace to fill the spaces where the temptations once existed:

Fill me with Your love and renew my spirit, Lord. I pray for blessings upon those who have caused temptation and ask for Your guidance as I move forward, free and whole.

Declaration of God's Strength (10 Minutes): Speak aloud declarations of God's strength over your life:

I declare that I am filled with the strength of God to overcome all temptations (see 1 Corinthians 10:13). *I trust in God's perfect plan for my life* (see Jeremiah 29:11). *I am steadfast and secure in His love* (see James 1:12).

Closing (5 Minutes): End your prayer with thanksgiving and trust:

Thank You, Lord, for hearing my prayer. I trust in Your power and grace. Amen!

Now, take a moment to breathe deeply, feeling the peace within.

— PRAYING FOR YOUR CITY —

Praying for your city can be a powerful way to seek blessings, protection, and guidance for your community.

Preparation (5 Minutes): Start your prayer time by creating a quiet and reflective space by playing calming music or sitting in silence.

Invocation (5 Minutes): Ask for divine guidance and protection during this prayer:

Heavenly Father, in Jesus' name I come before You with an open heart, seeking Your strength and wisdom. I ask You, Holy Spirit, to guide me and for Your protection during this time of reflection and renewal.

Praise and Worship (5 Minutes): Begin by praising God for His sovereignty and goodness. Sing worship songs or declare His attributes aloud. This invites His presence and sets the atmosphere for prayer:

Enter his gates with thanksgiving and his courts with praise; give thanks to him and praise his name. Psalm 100:4

Confession and Repentance (10 Minutes): Confess any personal or communal sins that might hinder your prayer. Ask for forgiveness and the cleansing power of the blood of Jesus over yourself and the city:

If we confess our sins, he is faithful and just and will forgive us our sins and purify us from all un-righteousness. 1 John 1:9

Scripture Reading (10 Minutes): Read and meditate on scriptures that speak of God's promises and blessings for cities and communities:

Also, seek the peace and prosperity of the city to which I have carried you into exile. Pray to the LORD for it, because if it prospers, you too will prosper. Jeremiah 29:7

Unless the LORD builds the house, the builders labor in vain. Unless the LORD watches over the city, the guards stand watch in vain. Psalm 127:1

Intercession (10 Minutes): Pray for the leaders, residents, and specific needs of your city. Lift up issues such as safety, unity, economic stability, and spiritual revival:

I urge, then, first of all, that petitions, prayers, intercession and thanksgiving be made for all people. 1 Timothy 2:1

Declaration of God's Authority (5 Minutes): Proclaim God's ownership and authority over the city. Declare that Jesus is Lord over the land, and renounce any claim the enemy might have:

109

The earth is the LORD's, and everything in it, the world, and all who live in it. Psalm 24:1

Renewal and Blessing (5 Minutes): Invite divine love and peace to fill the city. Pray for blessings upon the residents and ask for God's guidance as the city moves forward:

Fill me with Your love and renew my spirit, Lord. I pray for blessings upon the city and ask for Your guidance as we move forward, free and whole.

Closing (5 Minutes): End your prayer with thanksgiving and trust:

Thank You, Lord, for hearing my prayer. I trust in Your power and grace. Amen!

Now, take a moment to breathe deeply, feeling the peace within.

— PRAYING FOR THE GOVERNMENT —

Prayer for the government can be a powerful way to seek blessings, wisdom, and guidance for leaders and officials.

Preparation (5 Minutes): Start by creating a quiet and reflective space. Play calming music or sit in silence.

Invocation (5 Minutes): Ask for divine guidance and protection during this prayer:

Heavenly Father, in Jesus' name I come before You with an open heart, seeking Your strength and wisdom. I ask You, Holy Spirit, to guide me and for Your protection during this time of reflection and renewal.

Praise and Worship (5 Minutes): Begin by praising God for His sovereignty and goodness. Sing worship

songs or declare His attributes aloud. This invites His presence and sets the atmosphere for prayer:

Enter his gates with thanksgiving and his courts with praise; give thanks to him and praise his name. Psalm 100:4

Confession and Repentance (5 Minutes): Confess any personal or communal sins that might hinder prayer. Ask for forgiveness and the cleansing power of the blood of Jesus over yourself and the government:

If we confess our sins, he is faithful and just and will forgive us our sins and purify us from all un-righteousness. 1 John 1:9

Scripture Reading (10 Minutes): Read and meditate on scriptures that speak of God's promises and blessings for leaders and governments:

Let everyone be subject to the governing authorities, for there is no authority except that which God has established. The authorities that exist have been established by God. Romans 13:1

I urge, then, first of all, that petitions, prayers, intercession and thanksgiving be made for all people—for kings and all those in authority, that we may live peaceful and quiet lives in all godliness and holiness. 1 Timothy 2:1-2

Intercession (10 Minutes): Pray for the leaders, officials, and specific needs of the government. Lift up issues such as wisdom, integrity, justice, and unity:

I urge, then, first of all, that petitions, prayers, intercession and thanksgiving be made for all people. 1 Timothy 2:1

Declaration of God's Authority (10 Minutes): Proclaim God's ownership and authority over the government. Declare that Jesus is Lord over the land, and renounce any claim the enemy might have:

The earth is the LORD's, and everything in it, the world, and all who live in it. Psalm 24:1

Renewal and Blessing (5 Minutes): Invite divine love and peace to fill the government. Pray for blessings upon the leaders and ask for God's guidance as they move forward:

Fill me with Your love and renew my spirit, Lord. I pray for blessings upon the government and ask for Your guidance as we move forward, free and whole.

Closing (5 Minutes): End your prayer with thanksgiving and trust:

Thank You, Lord, for hearing my prayer. I trust in Your power and grace. Amen!

Now, Take a moment to breathe deeply, feeling the peace within.

— PRAYING FOR THE SALVATION OF YOUR FAMILY —

Prayer for the salvation of your family can be a powerful way to seek divine intervention and blessings.

Preparation (5 Minutes): Start by creating a quiet and reflective space. Play calming music or sit in silence.

Invocation (5 Minutes): Ask for divine guidance and protection during this prayer:

Heavenly Father, in Jesus' name I come before You with an open heart, seeking Your strength and wisdom. I ask You, Holy Spirit, to guide me and for Your protection during this time of reflection and renewal.

Praise and Worship (10 Minutes): Begin by praising God for His sovereignty and goodness. Sing worship

songs or declare His attributes aloud. This invites His presence and sets the atmosphere for prayer:

Enter his gates with thanksgiving and his courts with praise; give thanks to him and praise his name. Psalm 100:4

Confession and Repentance (10 Minutes): Confess any personal or communal sins that might hinder prayer. Ask for forgiveness and the cleansing power of the blood of Jesus over yourself and your family:

If we confess our sins, he is faithful and just and will forgive us our sins and purify us from all unrighteousness. 1 John 1:9

Scripture Reading (10 Minutes): Read and meditate on scriptures that speak of God's promises and blessings for salvation:

Believe in the Lord Jesus, and you will be saved—you and your household. Acts 16:31

If you declare with your mouth, "Jesus is Lord," and believe in your heart that God raised him from the dead, you will be saved. Romans 10:9

Intercession (5 Minutes): Pray for the salvation of your family members. Lift up their names and specific needs, asking God to touch their hearts and draw them closer to Himself:

I urge, then, first of all, that petitions, prayers, intercession and thanksgiving be made for all people.
1 Timothy 2:1

Declaration of God's Authority (5 Minutes): Proclaim God's ownership and authority over your family. Declare that Jesus is Lord over your household, and renounce any claim the enemy might have:

The earth is the LORD's, and everything in it, the world, and all who live in it. Psalm 24:1

Renewal and Blessing (5 Minutes): Invite divine love and peace to fill your family. Pray for blessings upon each family member and ask for God's guidance as they move forward:

Fill me with Your love and renew my spirit, Lord. I pray for blessings upon my family and ask for Your guidance as we move forward, free and whole.

Closing (5 Minutes): End your prayer with thanksgiving and trust:

Thank You, Lord, for hearing my prayer. I trust in Your power and grace. Amen!

Now, take a moment to breathe deeply, feeling the peace within.

— PRAYING FOR THE HOMELESS —

Praying for the homeless can be a powerful way to seek blessings, protection, and guidance for those in need.

Preparation (5 Minutes): Start by creating a quiet and reflective space. Play calming music or sit in silence.

Invocation (5 Minutes): Ask for divine guidance and protection during this prayer:

Heavenly Father, in Jesus' name I come before You with an open heart, seeking Your strength and wisdom. I ask You, Holy Spirit, to guide me and for Your protection during this time of reflection and renewal.

Praise and Worship (5 Minutes): Begin by praising God for His sovereignty and goodness. Sing worship

songs or declare His attributes aloud. This invites His presence and sets the atmosphere for prayer:

Enter his gates with thanksgiving and his courts with praise; give thanks to him and praise his name.   Psalm 100:4

Confession and Repentance (5 Minutes): Confess any personal or communal sins that might hinder prayer. Ask for forgiveness and the cleansing power of the blood of Jesus over yourself and the homeless:

If we confess our sins, he is faithful and just and will forgive us our sins and purify us from all un-righteousness.   1 John 1:9

Scripture Reading (10 Minutes): Read and meditate on scriptures that speak of God's promises and blessings for the homeless:

This poor man called, and the LORD *heard him; he saved him out of all his troubles.*   Psalm 34:6

For I was hungry and you gave me something to eat, I was thirsty and you gave me something to drink, I was a stranger and you invited me in, I needed clothes and you clothed me, I was sick and you looked after me, I was in prison and you came to visit me.   Matthew 25:35-36

Intercession (10 Minutes): Pray for the homeless, lifting up their specific needs such as shelter, food, safety, and spiritual revival:

I urge, then, first of all, that petitions, prayers, intercession and thanksgiving be made for all people.
1 Timothy 2:1

Declaration of God's Authority (10 Minutes): Proclaim God's ownership and authority over the lives of the homeless. Declare that Jesus is Lord over their circumstances, and renounce any claim the enemy might have:

The earth is the LORD's, and everything in it, the world, and all who live in it.   Psalm 24:1

Renewal and Blessing (5 Minutes): Invite divine love and peace to fill the lives of the homeless. Pray for blessings upon them and ask for God's guidance as they move forward:

Fill me with Your love and renew my spirit, Lord. I pray for blessings upon the homeless and ask for Your guidance as they move forward, free and whole.

Closing (5 Minutes): End your prayer with thanksgiving and trust:

Thank You, Lord, for hearing my prayer. I trust in Your power and grace. Amen!

Now, take a moment to breathe deeply, feeling the peace within.

—PRAYING FOR SPIRITUAL LEADERS —

Preparation (5 Minutes): Start by creating a quiet and reflective space. Play calming music or sit in silence. Begin with a deep breath, centering yourself.

Invocation (5 Minutes): Ask for divine guidance and protection during this prayer:

Heavenly Father, I come before You with an open heart, seeking Your strength and wisdom. I ask You, Holy Spirit, to guide me and for Your protection during this time of reflection and renewal.

Praise and Worship (10 Minutes): Begin by praising God for His sovereignty and goodness. Sing worship

songs or declare His attributes aloud. This invites His presence and sets the atmosphere for prayer:

Enter his gates with thanksgiving and his courts with praise; give thanks to him and praise his name.   Psalm 100:4

Confession and Repentance (5 Minutes): Confess any personal or communal sins that might hinder prayer. Ask for forgiveness and the cleansing power of the blood of Jesus over yourself and the spiritual leaders:

If we confess our sins, he is faithful and just and will forgive us our sins and purify us from all unrighteousness.   1 John 1:9

Scripture Reading (10 Minutes): Read and meditate on scriptures that speak of God's promises and blessings for spiritual leaders:

Here is a trustworthy saying: Whoever aspires to be an overseer desires a noble task. Now the overseer is to be above reproach, faithful to his wife, temperate, self-controlled, respectable, hospitable, able to teach, not given to drunkenness, not violent but gentle, not quarrelsome, not a lover of money. He must manage his own family well and see that his children obey him, and he must do so in a manner worthy of full respect. (If anyone does not know how to manage his own family, how can he take care of God's church?) He must not be a recent convert, or he may become conceited and fall under the same judgment as the devil. He must also have a good reputation with outsiders, so that he will not fall into disgrace and into the devil's trap."

1 Timothy 3:1-7

Since an overseer manages God's household, he must be blameless—not overbearing, not quick-tempered, not given to drunkenness, not violent, not pursuing dishonest gain. Rather, he must be hospitable, one who loves what is good, who is self-controlled, upright, holy and disciplined. He must hold firmly to the trustworthy message as it

has been taught, so that he can encourage others by sound doctrine and refute those who oppose it.
Titus 1:7-9

Intercession (10 Minutes): Pray for the spiritual leaders, lifting their specific needs such as wisdom, integrity, strength, and spiritual revival:

I urge, then, first of all, that petitions, prayers, intercession and thanksgiving be made for all people
.
1 Timothy 2:1

Declaration of God's Authority (5 Minutes): Proclaim God's ownership and authority over the spiritual leaders. Declare that Jesus is Lord over their lives and ministries, and renounce any claim the enemy might have:

The earth is the LORD's, and everything in it, the world, and all who live in it.   Psalm 24:1

Renewal and Blessing (5 Minutes): Invite divine love and peace to fill the spiritual leaders. Pray for blessings upon them and ask for God's guidance as they move forward:

Fill me with Your love and renew my spirit, Lord. I pray for blessings upon the spiritual leaders and ask for Your guidance as they move forward, free and whole.

Closing (5 Minutes): End your prayer with thanksgiving and trust:

Thank You, Lord, for hearing my prayer. I trust in Your power and grace. Amen!

Now, take a moment to listen for the voice of God, feeling the peace within.

— PRAYING FOR THE CONVERSION OF LEADERS IN AUTHORITY AND INFLUENCE —

Preparation (5 Minutes): Start by creating a quiet and reflective space. Invite the Holy Spirit by playing calming music or sitting in silence.

Invocation (5 Minutes): Ask for divine guidance and protection during this prayer:

Heavenly Father, in Jesus name I come before You with an open heart, seeking Your strength and wisdom. I ask You, Holy Spirit, to guide me and for Your protection during this time of reflection and renewal.

Praise and Worship (5 Minutes): Begin by praising God for His sovereignty and goodness. Sing worship

songs or declare His attributes aloud. This invites His presence and sets the atmosphere for prayer:

Enter his gates with thanksgiving and his courts with praise; give thanks to him and praise his name. Psalm 100:4

Confession and Repentance (5 Minutes): Confess any personal or communal sins that might hinder prayer. Ask for forgiveness and the cleansing power of the blood of Jesus over yourself and the leaders:

If we confess our sins, he is faithful and just and will forgive us our sins and purify us from all unrighteousness. 1 John 1:9

Scripture Reading (10 Minutes): Read and meditate on scriptures that speak of God's promises and blessings for leaders and their conversion:

Let everyone be subject to the governing authorities, for there is no authority except that which God has established. The authorities that exist have been established by God. Romans 13:1

I urge, then, first of all, that petitions, prayers, intercession and thanksgiving be made for all people—for kings and all those in authority, that we may live peaceful and quiet lives in all godliness and holiness. 1 Timothy 2:1-2

Intercession (10 Minutes): Pray for the leaders, officials, and specific needs of the government. Lift up issues such as wisdom, integrity, justice, and unity:

I urge, then, first of all, that petitions, prayers, intercession and thanksgiving be made for all people. 1 Timothy 2:1

Declaration of God's Authority (10 Minutes): Proclaim God's ownership and authority over the leaders. Declare that Jesus is Lord over their lives and ministries, and renounce any claim the enemy might have:

The earth is the LORD's, *and everything in it, the world, and all who live in it.*   Psalm 24:1

Renewal and Blessing (5 Minutes): Invite divine love and peace to fill the leaders. Pray for blessings upon them and ask for God's guidance as they move forward:

Fill me with Your love and renew my spirit, Lord. I pray for blessings upon the leaders and ask for Your guidance as they move forward, free and whole.

Closing (5 Minutes): End your prayer with thanksgiving and trust:

Thank You, Lord, for hearing my prayer. I trust in Your power and grace. Amen!

Now, take a moment to listen for the voice of God, feeling the peace within.

— PRAYING FOR THE UNEVANGELIZED —

Preparation (5 Minutes): Start by creating a quiet and reflective space. Invite the Holy Spirit by playing calming music or sitting in silence. Begin with a deep breath.

Invocation (5 Minutes): Ask for divine guidance and protection during this prayer:

Heavenly Father, in Jesus' name I come before You with an open heart, seeking Your strength and wisdom. I ask You, Holy Spirit, to guide me and for Your protection during this time of reflection and renewal.

Praise and Worship (5 Minutes): Begin by praising God for His sovereignty and goodness. Sing worship songs or declare His attributes aloud. This invites His presence and sets the atmosphere for prayer:

Enter his gates with thanksgiving and his courts with praise; give thanks to him and praise his name.   Psalm 100:4

Confession and Repentance (10 Minutes): Confess any personal or communal sins that might hinder prayer. Ask for forgiveness and the cleansing power of the blood of Jesus over yourself and the unevangelized:

If we confess our sins, he is faithful and just and will forgive us our sins and purify us from all un-righteousness.   1 John 1:9

Scripture Reading (10 Minutes): Read and meditate on scriptures that speak of God's promises and blessings for the unevangelized:

Therefore go and make disciples of all nations, baptizing them in the name of the Father and of the Son and of the Holy Spirit, and teaching them to obey everything I have commanded you. And surely I am with you always, to the very end of the age.   Matthew 28:19-20

How, then, can they call on the one they have not believed in? And how can they believe in the one of whom they have not heard? And how can they hear without someone preaching to them? And how can anyone preach unless they are sent? As it is written: "How beautiful are the feet of those who bring good news!" Romans 10:14-15

Intercession (10 Minutes): Pray for the unevangelized, lifting up their specific needs, such as spiritual awakening, protection, and provision:

I urge, then, first of all, that petitions, prayers, intercession and thanksgiving be made for all people. 1 Timothy 2:1

Declaration of God's Authority (15 Minutes): This is a powerful time to speak God's truth aloud and align your heart with His mission for the nations. These declarations are rooted in the Scriptures. Speak them out slowly, prayerfully, and WITH POWER!

Proclaiming God's Sovereignty, Power, and Desire to Reach All Peoples:

Declaration 1: GOD REIGNS OVER ALL NATIONS

The LORD has established his throne in heaven, and his kingdom rules over all. Psalm 103:19

Say aloud and demonstratively:

God, You reign over every tribe, nation, and tongue. No place is beyond Your reach, and no people are forgotten by You!

Declaration 2: THE EARTH BELONGS TO THE LORD

The earth is the LORD's, and everything in it, the world, and all who live in it. Psalm 24:1

Say aloud and demonstratively:

Every person, every land, every soul belongs to You, Lord. You are the rightful King of all the earth!

Declaration 3: GOD DESIRES ALL TO BE SAVED

[God] wants all people to be saved and to come to a knowledge of the truth. 1 Timothy 2:4

Say aloud and demonstratively:

It is Your will, Lord that none should perish. I declare that unreached people groups will come to know You!

Declaration 4: GOD'S WORD WILL NOT RETURN VOID

So is my word that goes out from my mouth: it will not return to me empty, but will accomplish what I desire. Isaiah 55:11

Say aloud and demonstratively:

Your Word has power to penetrate every heart and culture. I declare that the Gospel will bear fruit in even the most remote places!

Declaration 5: JESUS HAS ALL AUTHORITY

All authority in heaven and on earth has been given to me. Therefore, go and make disciples of all nations ... .   Matthew 28:18-19

Say aloud and demonstratively:

Jesus, You are the King of kings. I declare Your authority over closed nations, resistant hearts, and spiritual strongholds!

Declaration 6: THE GATES OF HELL WILL NOT PREVAIL

I will build my church, and the gates of Hades will not overcome it.   Matthew 16:18

Say aloud and demonstratively:

I declare that the Church will rise in power, and no demonic force will stop the spread of the Gospel!

DECLARATION 7: THE GLORY OF GOD WILL FILL THE EARTH

For the earth will be filled with the knowledge of the glory of the LORD as the waters cover the sea.

Habakkuk 2:14

Say aloud and demonstratively:

I declare that the knowledge of God will flood the earth. Every nation will witness Your glory, Lord!

Declaration 8: God Is SENDING WORKERS INTO THE HARVEST

Ask the Lord of the harvest, therefore, to send out workers into his harvest field.

Matthew 9:38

Say aloud and demonstratively:

I declare that laborers are being raised up and sent to the unreached and will be equipped, anointed, and fearless!

Suggested Activity: As you declare the Word, consider walking around your room or neighborhood, using a globe, world map, or your phone to visually pray over nations or people groups. Speak these truths while touching or pointing to different regions.

— PRAYING STRATEGIES FOR CHANGING NATIONS —

Preparation (5 Minutes): Start by creating a quiet space. Invite the Holy Spirit, play calming music, or sit in silence.

Invocation (5 Minutes): Ask for divine guidance and protection during this prayer:

Heavenly Father, in Jesus' name I come before You with an open heart, seeking Your strength and wisdom. I ask You, Holy Spirit, to guide me and for Your protection during this time of reflection and renewal.

Praise and Worship (10 Minutes): Begin by praising God for His sovereignty and goodness. Sing worship songs or declare His attributes aloud. This invites His presence and sets the atmosphere for prayer:

Enter his gates with thanksgiving and his courts with praise; give thanks to him and praise his name.   Psalm 100:4

Confession and Repentance (10 Minutes): Confess any personal or communal sins that might hinder prayer. Ask for forgiveness and the cleansing power of the blood of Jesus over yourself and the nation/s:

If we confess our sins, he is faithful and just and will forgive us our sins and purify us from all un-righteousness.   1 John 1:9

Scripture Reading (5 Minutes): Read and meditate on scriptures that speak of God's promises and blessings for nations:

Also, seek the peace and prosperity of the city to which I have carried you into exile. Pray to the LORD for it, because if it prospers, you too will prosper.   Jeremiah 29:7

Blessed is the nation whose God is the LORD, the people he chose for his inheritance.   Psalm 33:12

Intercession (5 Minutes): Pray for the leaders, residents, and specific needs of the nation. Lift up issues such as safety, unity, economic stability, and spiritual revival:

I urge, then, first of all, that petitions, prayers, intercession and thanksgiving be made for all people.
1 Timothy 2:1

Declaration of God's Authority (10 Minutes): Proclaim God's ownership and authority over the nation. Declare that Jesus is Lord over the land and renounce any claim the enemy might have:

The earth is the LORD's, and everything in it, the world, and all who live in it.   Psalm 24:1

Renewal and Blessing (5 Minutes): Invite divine love and peace to fill the nation. Pray for blessings upon the residents and ask for God's guidance as the nation moves forward:

Fill me with Your love and renew my spirit, Lord. I pray for blessings upon the nation and ask for Your guidance as we move forward, free and whole.

Closing (5 Minutes): End your prayer with thanksgiving and trust:

Thank You, Lord, for hearing my prayer. I trust in Your power and grace. Amen!

Now, take a moment to listen for the voice of God, feeling the peace within.

— PRAYING FOR SOMEONE CLOSE TO YOU BUT FAR FROM GOD —

Preparation (5 Minutes): Start by creating a quiet and reflective space. Invite the Holy Spirit, play calming music, or sit in silence. Begin with a deep breath.

Invocation (5 Minutes): Ask for divine guidance and protection during this prayer:

Heavenly Father, in Jesus' name I come before You with an open heart, seeking Your strength and wisdom. I ask You, Holy Spirit, to guide me and for Your protection during this time of reflection and renewal.

Praise and Worship (5 Minutes): Begin by praising God for His sovereignty and goodness. Sing worship songs or declare His attributes aloud. This invites His presence and sets the atmosphere for prayer:

Enter his gates with thanksgiving and his courts with praise; give thanks to him and praise his name. Psalm 100:4

Confession and Repentance (5 Minutes): Confess any personal or communal sins that might hinder prayer. Ask for forgiveness and the cleansing power of the blood of Jesus over yourself and the person you are praying for:

If we confess our sins, he is faithful and just and will forgive us our sins and purify us from all unrighteousness. 1 John 1:9

Scripture Reading (10 Minutes): Read and meditate on scriptures that speak of God's promises and blessings for those who are away from Him:

Suppose one of you has a hundred sheep and loses one of them. Doesn't he leave the ninety-nine in the open country and go after the lost sheep until he finds it? And when he finds it, he joyfully puts it on his shoulders and goes home. Then he calls his

145

friends and neighbors together and says, "Rejoice with me; I have found my lost sheep." I tell you that in the same way there will be more rejoicing in heaven over one sinner who repents than over ninety-nine righteous persons who do not need to repent. Luke 15:4-7

I will give them a heart to know me, that I am the Lord. *They will be my people, and I will be their God, for they will return to me with all their heart.* Jeremiah 24:7

Intercession (10 Minutes): Pray for the person who is away from God, lifting up their specific needs, such as spiritual awakening, protection, and provision:

I urge, then, first of all, that petitions, prayers, intercession and thanksgiving be made for all people. 1 Timothy 2:1

Declaration of God's Authority (10 Minutes): Proclaim God's ownership and authority over the person's life. Declare that Jesus is Lord over their circumstances and renounce any claim the enemy might have:

*The earth is the L*ORD*'s, and everything in it, the world, and all who live in it.* Psalm 24:1

Renewal and Blessing (5 Minutes): Invite divine love and peace to fill the person's life. Pray for blessings upon them and ask for God's guidance as they move forward:

Fill me with Your love and renew my spirit, Lord. I pray for blessings upon [person's name] *and ask for Your guidance as they move forward, free and whole.*

Closing (5 Minutes): End your prayer with thanksgiving and trust:

Thank You, Lord, for hearing my prayer. I trust in Your power and grace. Amen!

Now, take a moment to listen to the voice of God, feeling the peace within.

— PRAYING FOR THIS GENERATION OF YOUTH AND CHILDREN —

Preparation (5 Minutes): Start by creating a quiet and reflective space. Invite the Holy Spirit, play calming music, or sit in silence. Begin with a deep breath.

Invocation (5 Minutes): Ask for divine guidance and protection during this prayer:

Heavenly Father, in Jesus' name I come before You with an open heart, seeking Your strength and wisdom. I ask You, Holy Spirit, to guide me and for Your protection during this time of reflection and renewal.

Praise and Worship (5 Minutes): Begin by praising God for His sovereignty and goodness. Sing worship songs or declare His attributes aloud. This invites His presence and sets the atmosphere for prayer:

Enter his gates with thanksgiving and his courts with praise; give thanks to him and praise his name. Psalm 100:4

Confession and Repentance (5 Minutes): Confess any personal or communal sins that might hinder prayer. Ask for forgiveness and the cleansing power of the blood of Jesus over yourself and the youth and children:

If we confess our sins, he is faithful and just and will forgive us our sins and purify us from all un-righteousness. 1 John 1:9

Scripture Reading (10 Minutes): Read and meditate on scriptures that speak of God's promises and blessings for youth and children:

"For I know the plans I have for you," declares the Lord, *"plans to prosper you and not to harm you, plans to give you hope and a future."* Jeremiah 29:11

Children are a heritage from the LORD, offspring a reward from him.   Psalm 127:3

Intercession (10 Minutes): Pray for the youth and children, lifting up their specific needs such as safety, education, emotional well-being, and spiritual revival:

I urge, then, first of all, that petitions, prayers, intercession and thanksgiving be made for all people.
                    1 Timothy 2:1

Declaration of God's Authority (10 Minutes): Proclaim God's ownership and authority over the lives of the youth and children. Declare that Jesus is Lord over their circumstances and renounce any claim the enemy might have:

The earth is the LORD's, and everything in it, the world, and all who live in it.   Psalm 24:1

Renewal and Blessing (5 Minutes): Invite divine love and peace to fill the lives of the youth and children.

Pray for blessings upon them and ask for God's guidance as they move forward:

Fill me with Your love and renew my spirit, Lord. I pray for blessings upon the youth and children and ask for Your guidance as they move forward, free and whole.

Closing (5 Minutes): End your prayer with thanksgiving and trust:

Thank You, Lord, for hearing my prayer. I trust in Your power and grace. Amen!

Now, take a moment to breathe deeply, feeling the peace within.

— PRAYING FOR A BROKEN RELATIONSHIP —

Preparation (5 Minutes): Start by creating a quiet and reflective space. Invite the Holy Spirit, play calming music, or sit in silence.

Invocation (5 Minutes): Ask for divine guidance and protection during this prayer:

Heavenly Father, in Jesus' name I come before You with an open heart, seeking Your strength and wisdom. I ask You, Holy Spirit, to guide me and for Your protection during this time of reflection and renewal.

Praise and Worship (10 Minutes): Begin by praising God for His sovereignty and goodness. Sing worship songs or declare His attributes aloud. This invites His presence and sets the atmosphere for prayer:

Enter his gates with thanksgiving and his courts with praise; give thanks to him and praise his name. Psalm 100:4

Confession and Repentance (10 Minutes): Confess any personal or relational sins that might hinder prayer. Ask for forgiveness and the cleansing power of the blood of Jesus over yourself and the relationship:

If we confess our sins, he is faithful and just and will forgive us our sins and purify us from all un-righteousness. 1 John 1:9

Scripture Reading (5 Minutes): Read and meditate on scriptures that speak of God's promises and blessings for relationships:

Be kind and compassionate to one another, forgiving each other, just as in Christ God forgave you. Ephesians 4:32

Bear with each other and forgive one another if any of you have a grievance against someone. Forgive as the Lord forgave you. Colossians 3:13

Intercession (5 Minutes): Pray for the broken relationship, lifting up specific needs such as healing, forgiveness, and restoration:

I urge, then, first of all, that petitions, prayers, intercession and thanksgiving be made for all people. 1 Timothy 2:1

Declaration of God's Authority (10 Minutes): Proclaim God's ownership and authority over the relationship. Declare that Jesus is Lord over the circumstances and renounce any claim the enemy might have:

The earth is the LORD's, and everything in it, the world, and all who live in it. Psalm 24:1

Renewal and Blessing (5 Minutes): Invite divine love and peace to fill the relationship. Pray for blessings upon both parties and ask for God's guidance as they move forward:

Fill me with Your love and renew my spirit, Lord. I pray for blessings upon [person's name] and ask for Your guidance as we move forward, free and whole.

Closing (5 Minutes): End your prayer with thanksgiving and trust:

Thank You, Lord, for hearing my prayer. I trust in Your power and grace. Amen!

Now, take a moment to breathe deeply, feeling the peace within.

— PRAYING AGAINST SCHOOL VIOLENCE —

Preparation (5 Minutes): Start by creating a quiet and reflective space. Invite the Holy Spirit, play calming music, or sit in silence. Begin with a deep breath.

Invocation (5 Minutes): Ask for divine guidance and protection during this prayer:

Heavenly Father, in Jesus' name I come before You with an open heart, seeking Your strength and wisdom. I ask You, Holy Spirit, to guide me and for Your protection during this time of reflection and renewal.

Praise and Worship (10 Minutes): Begin by praising God for His sovereignty and goodness. Sing worship songs or declare His attributes aloud. This invites His presence and sets the atmosphere for prayer:

Enter his gates with thanksgiving and his courts with praise; give thanks to him and praise his name. Psalm 100:4

Confession and Repentance (5 Minutes): Confess any personal or communal sins that might hinder prayer. Ask for forgiveness and the cleansing power of the blood of Jesus over yourself and the school community:

If we confess our sins, he is faithful and just and will forgive us our sins and purify us from all unrighteousness. 1 John 1:9

Scripture Reading (10 Minutes): Read and meditate on scriptures that speak of God's protection and promises:

I will say of the LORD, "He is my refuge and my fortress, my God, in whom I trust." Psalm 91:2

No weapon forged against you will prevail, and you will refute every tongue that accuses you. Isaiah 54:17

157

Intercession (5 Minutes): Pray for the students, teachers, and staff, lifting up their specific needs such as safety, emotional well-being, and spiritual revival:

I urge, then, first of all, that petitions, prayers, intercession and thanksgiving be made for all people.
                                                    1 Timothy 2:1

Declaration of God's Authority (10 Minutes): Proclaim God's ownership and authority over the school. Declare that Jesus is Lord over the land and renounce any claim the enemy might have:

The earth is the LORD's, and everything in it, the world, and all who live in it.   Psalm 24:1

Renewal and Blessing (5 Minutes): Invite divine love and peace to fill the school. Pray for blessings upon the students, teachers, and staff, and ask for God's guidance as they move forward:

Fill me with Your love and renew my spirit, Lord. I pray for blessings upon the school and ask for Your guidance as we move forward, free and whole.

Closing (5 Minutes): End your prayer with thanksgiving and trust:

Thank You, Lord, for hearing my prayer. I trust in Your power and grace. Amen!

Now, take a moment just to SIT in God's presence, feeling the peace within.

— PRAYING AGAINST SPIRITUAL NETWORKS OF WICKEDNESS —

Preparation (5 Minutes): Start by creating a quiet and reflective space. Invite the Holy Spirit, play calming music, or sit in silence.

Invocation (5 Minutes): Ask for divine guidance and protection during this prayer:

Heavenly Father, in Jesus' name I come before You with an open heart, seeking Your strength and wisdom. I ask You, Holy Spirit, to guide me and for Your protection during this time of reflection and renewal.

Praise and Worship (5 Minutes): Begin by praising God for His sovereignty and goodness. Sing worship songs or declare His attributes aloud. This invites His presence and sets the atmosphere for prayer:

Enter his gates with thanksgiving and his courts with praise; give thanks to him and praise his name. Psalm 100:4

Confession and Repentance (5 Minutes): Confess any personal or communal sins that might hinder prayer. Ask for forgiveness and the cleansing power of the blood of Jesus over yourself and the community:

If we confess our sins, he is faithful and just and will forgive us our sins and purify us from all un-righteousness. 1 John 1:9

Scripture Reading (10 Minutes): Read and meditate on scriptures that speak of God's protection and promises:

I will say of the LORD, "He is my refuge and my fortress, my God, in whom I trust." Psalm 91:2

No weapon forged against you will prevail, and you will refute every tongue that accuses you.
Isaiah 54:17

Intercession (10 Minutes): Pray for the community, lifting up their specific needs, such as safety, emotional well-being, and spiritual revival:

I urge, then, first of all, that petitions, prayers, intercession and thanksgiving be made for all people.
1 Timothy 2:1

Declaration of God's Authority (5 Minutes): Proclaim God's ownership and authority over the community. Declare that Jesus is Lord over the land, and renounce any claim the enemy might have:

The earth is the LORD's, and everything in it, the world, and all who live in it. Psalm 24:1

Renewal and Blessing (10 Minutes): Invite divine love and peace to fill the community. Pray for blessings upon the residents and ask for God's guidance as they move forward:

Fill me with Your love and renew my spirit, Lord. I pray for blessings upon the community and ask for Your guidance as we move forward, free and whole.

Closing (5 Minutes): End your prayer with thanksgiving and trust:

Thank You, Lord, for hearing my prayer. I trust in Your power and grace. Amen!

— PRAYING TO RELEASE ANGELS TO WORK FOR YOU —

Preparation (5 Minutes: Start by creating a quiet and reflective space. Invite the Holy Spirit, play calming music, or sit in silence.

Invocation (5 Minutes): Ask for divine guidance and protection during this prayer:

Heavenly Father, in Jesus' name I come before You with an open heart, seeking Your strength and wisdom. I ask You, Holy Spirit, to guide me and for Your protection during this time of reflection and renewal.

Praise and Worship (5 Minutes): Begin by praising God for His sovereignty and goodness. Sing worship songs or declare His attributes aloud. This invites His presence and sets the atmosphere for prayer:

Enter his gates with thanksgiving and his courts with praise; give thanks to him and praise his name. Psalm 100:4

Confession and Repentance (5 Minutes): Confess any personal or communal sins that might hinder prayer. Ask for forgiveness and the cleansing power of the blood of Jesus over yourself and the community:

If we confess our sins, he is faithful and just and will forgive us our sins and purify us from all un-righteousness. 1 John 1:9

Scripture Reading (10 Minutes): Read and meditate on scriptures that speak of God's promises and blessings:

For he will command his angels concerning you to guard you in all your ways. Psalm 91:11

Are not all angels ministering spirits sent to serve those who will inherit salvation? Hebrews 1:14

Intercession (10 Minutes): Pray for the release of angels to work on your behalf, lifting up specific needs, such as protection, guidance, and provision:

I urge, then, first of all, that petitions, prayers, intercession and thanksgiving be made for all people.
1 Timothy 2:1

Declaration of God's Authority (10 Minutes): Proclaim God's ownership and authority over your life. Declare that Jesus is Lord over your circumstances and renounce any claim the enemy might have:

The earth is the LORD's, and everything in it, the world, and all who live in it. Psalm 24:1

Renewal and Blessing (5 Minutes): Invite divine love and peace to fill your life. Pray for blessings upon yourself and ask for God's guidance as you move forward:

Fill me with Your love and renew my spirit, Lord. I pray for blessings upon my life and ask for Your guidance as I move forward, free and whole.

Closing (5 Minutes): End your prayer with thanksgiving and trust:

Thank You, Lord, for hearing my prayer. I trust in Your power and grace. Amen!

Now, take a moment to listen to the voice of God, feeling the peace within.

— PRAYING, ENGAGING THE NORTH WIND —

Preparation (5 Minutes): Start by creating a quiet space. Invite the Holy Spirit, play calming music, or sit in silence.

Invocation (5 Minutes): Ask for divine guidance and protection during this prayer:

Heavenly Father, in Jesus' name I come before You with an open heart, seeking Your strength and wisdom. I ask You, Holy Spirit, to guide me and for Your protection during this time of reflection and renewal.

Praise and Worship (10 Minutes): Begin by praising God for His sovereignty and goodness. Sing worship songs or declare His attributes aloud. This invites His presence and sets the atmosphere for prayer:

Enter his gates with thanksgiving and his courts with praise; give thanks to him and praise his name.   Psalm 100:4

Confession and Repentance (5 Minutes): Confess any personal or communal sins that might hinder prayer. Ask for forgiveness and the cleansing power of the blood of Jesus over yourself and the community:

If we confess our sins, he is faithful and just and will forgive us our sins and purify us from all un-righteousness."   1 John 1:9

Scripture Reading (5 Minutes): Read and meditate on scriptures that speak of God's promises and blessings:

The north wind brings forth rain: so doth an angry countenance a backbiting tongue.
                                                  Proverbs 25:23, KJV

As I looked, behold, a storm wind was coming from the north.   Ezekiel 1:4, NASB

Awake, O north wind; and come, thou south; blow upon my garden, that the spices thereof may flow out. Let my beloved come into his garden and eat his pleasant fruits.   Song of Solomon 4:16, KJV

Intercession (10 Minutes): Pray for the north wind to drive away the rain of adversity, poverty, desperation, agents of darkness etc.

Declaration of God's Authority (10 Minutes): Proclaim God's ownership and authority over your life. Declare that Jesus is Lord over your circumstances and renounce any claim the enemy might have:

Fair weather cameth out of the north; with God is terrible majesty.   Job 37:22, KJV

Renewal and Blessing (5 Minutes): Invite the north wind to be a messenger of God's terrible majesty. Expect it to drive away rain. The strength with which the north wind drives away rain is the same strength and speed that the wind, used as a weapon, will drive away your enemies.

Closing (5 Minutes): End your prayer with thanksgiving and trust:

Thank You, Lord, for hearing my prayer. I trust in Your power and grace. Amen!

— PRAYING, ENGAGING THE SOUTH WIND —

Preparation (5 Minutes): Start by creating a quiet and reflective space. Invite the Holy Spirit, play calming music, or sit in silence.

Invocation (5 Minutes): Ask for divine guidance and protection during this prayer:

Heavenly Father, in Jesus' name I come before You with an open heart, seeking Your strength and wisdom. I ask You, Holy Spirit, to guide me and for Your protection during this time of reflection and renewal.

Praise and Worship (5 Minutes): Begin by praising God for His sovereignty and goodness. Sing worship songs or declare His attributes aloud. This invites His presence and sets the atmosphere for prayer:

Enter his gates with thanksgiving and his courts with praise; give thanks to him and praise his name. Psalm 100:4

Confession and Repentance (5 Minutes): Confess any personal or communal sins that might hinder prayer. Ask for forgiveness and the cleansing power of the blood of Jesus over yourself and the community:

If we confess our sins, he is faithful and just and will forgive us our sins and purify us from all un-righteousness. 1 John 1:9

Scripture Reading (10 Minutes): Read and meditate on scriptures that speak of God's promises and blessings:

How thy garments are warm, when he quieteth the earth by the south wind. Job 37:17, KJV

He caused an east wind to blow in the heaven: and by his power he brought in the south wind. Psalm 78:26, KJV

Awake, O north wind; and come, thou south; blow upon my garden, that the spices thereof may flow out. Let my beloved come into his garden and eat his pleasant fruits.   Song of Solomon 4:16, KJV

Intercession (10 Minutes): Pray for the South Wind to bring warmth, comfort, and blessings. Lift up specific needs, such as healing, provision, and spiritual revival:

I urge, then, first of all, that petitions, prayers, intercession and thanksgiving be made for all people.
1 Timothy 2:1

Declaration of God's Authority (10 Minutes): Proclaim God's ownership and authority over your life. Declare that Jesus is Lord over your circumstances, and renounce any claim the enemy might have:

The earth is the LORD's, and everything in it, the world, and all who live in it.   Psalm 24:1

Renewal and Blessing (5 Minutes): Invite the South Wind to bring renewal and blessings. Pray for divine love and peace to fill your life:

Fill me with Your love and renew my spirit, Lord. I pray for blessings upon my life and for Your guidance as I move forward, free and whole.

Closing (5 Minutes): End your prayer with thanksgiving and trust:

Thank You, Lord, for hearing my prayer. I trust in Your power and grace. Amen!

— PRAYING, ENGAGING THE EAST WIND —

Preparation (5 Minutes): Start by creating a quiet and reflective space. Invite the Holy Spirit, play calming music, or sit in silence. Begin with a deep breath.

Invocation (5 Minutes): Ask for divine guidance and protection during this prayer:

Heavenly Father, in Jesus' name I come before You with an open heart, seeking Your strength and wisdom. I ask You, Holy Spirit, to guide me and for Your protection during this time of reflection and renewal.

Praise and Worship (5 Minutes): Begin by praising God for His sovereignty and goodness. Sing worship songs or declare His attributes aloud. This invites His presence and sets the atmosphere for prayer:

Enter his gates with thanksgiving and his courts with praise; give thanks to him and praise his name. Psalm 100:4

Confession and Repentance (5 Minutes): Confess any personal or communal sins that might hinder prayer. Ask for forgiveness and the cleansing power of the blood of Jesus over yourself and the community:

If we confess our sins, he is faithful and just and will forgive us our sins and purify us from all unrighteousness. 1 John 1:9

Scripture Reading (10 Minutes): Read and meditate on scriptures that speak of God's promises and blessings:

And Moses stretched forth his rod over the land of Egypt, and the LORD brought an east wind upon the land all that day, and all that night; and when it was morning, the east wind brought the locusts. Exodus 10:13, KJV

Thou breakest the ships of Tarshish with an east wind. Psalm 48:7, KJV

Yea, behold, being planted, shall it prosper? shall it not utterly wither, when the east wind toucheth it? it shall wither in the furrows where it grew. Ezekiel 17:10, KJV

Intercession (10 Minutes): Pray for the East Wind to bring change, transformation, and blessings. Lift up specific needs, such as healing, provision, and spiritual revival:

I urge, then, first of all, that petitions, prayers, intercession and thanksgiving be made for all people. 1 Timothy 2:1

Declaration of God's Authority (10 Minutes): Proclaim God's ownership and authority over your life. Declare that Jesus is Lord over your circumstances and renounce any claim the enemy might have:

The earth is the LORD's, and everything in it, the world, and all who live in it.   Psalm 24:1

Renewal and Blessing (5 Minutes): Invite the East Wind to bring renewal and blessings. Pray for divine love and peace to fill your life:

Fill me with Your love and renew my spirit, Lord. I pray for blessings upon my life and ask for Your guidance as I move forward, free and whole.

Closing (5 Minutes): End your prayer with thanksgiving and trust:

Thank You, Lord, for hearing my prayer. I trust in Your power and grace. Amen!

— PRAYING, ENGAGING THE WEST WIND —

Preparation (5 Minutes): Start by creating a quiet and reflective space. Invite the Holy Spirit, play calming music, or sit in silence.

Invocation (5 Minutes): Ask for divine guidance and protection during this prayer:

Heavenly Father, in Jesus' name I come before You with an open heart, seeking Your strength and wisdom. I ask You, Holy Spirit, to guide me and for Your protection during this time of reflection and renewal.

Praise and Worship (10 Minutes): Begin by praising God for His sovereignty and goodness. Sing worship songs or declare His attributes aloud. This invites His presence and sets the atmosphere for prayer:

Enter his gates with thanksgiving and his courts with praise; give thanks to him and praise his name. Psalm 100:4

Confession and Repentance (10 Minutes): Confess any personal or communal sins that might hinder prayer. Ask for forgiveness and the cleansing power of the blood of Jesus over yourself and the community:

If we confess our sins, he is faithful and just and will forgive us our sins and purify us from all un-righteousness. 1 John 1:9

Scripture Reading (5 Minutes): Read and meditate on scriptures that speak of God's promises and blessings:

And the LORD turned a mighty strong west wind, which took away the locusts, and cast them into the Red Sea; there remained not one locust in all the coasts of Egypt. Exodus 10:19, KJV

For the commandeth, and raiseth the stormy wind, which lifteth up the waves thereof.
Psalm 107:25, KJV

By what way is the light parted, which scattereth the east wind upon the earth?   Job 38:24, KJV

Intercession (5 Minutes): Pray for the West Wind to bring change, transformation, and blessings. Lift up specific needs, such as healing, provision, and spiritual revival:

I urge, then, first of all, that petitions, prayers, intercession and thanksgiving be made for all people.
1 Timothy 2:1

Declaration of God's Authority (10 Minutes): Proclaim God's ownership and authority over your life. Declare that Jesus is Lord over your circumstances, and renounce any claim the enemy might have:

The earth is the LORD's, and everything in it, the world, and all who live in it.   Psalm 24:1

Renewal and Blessing (5 Minutes): Invite the West Wind to bring renewal and blessings. Pray for divine love and peace to fill your life:

Fill me with Your love and renew my spirit, Lord. I pray for blessings upon my life and ask for Your guidance as I move forward, free and whole.

Closing (5 Minutes): End your prayer with thanksgiving and trust:

Thank You, Lord, for hearing my prayer. I trust in Your power and grace. Amen!

Now, take a moment to listen for the voice of God, feeling the peace within.

— PRAYING FOR YOUR NEIGHBOR —

Praise and Thanksgiving (10 Minutes): Begin with praise and thanksgiving. Thank God for your neighbor's life and His love for them. Thank God for placing your neighbor near you. Acknowledge God's sovereignty and goodness. Thank Him for any positive qualities or moments shared:

Give thanks in all circumstances; for this is God's will for you in Christ Jesus.   1 Thessalonians 5:18

Suggested Activity: Write a brief note or card of encouragement or thanksgiving for your neighbor, even if you do not give it to them right away.

Intercede for Your Neighbor's Salvation and Spiritual Growth (10 Minutes): Pray for your neighbor's salvation (if they're not a believer), or for a deepening relationship with God (if they are a believer). Ask the Lord to open their heart to His truth. Pray they would encounter Jesus personally. If they're believers, pray for their spiritual growth and discipleship:

Brothers and sisters, my heart's desire and prayed to God for the Israelites is that they may be saved.
                                                                    Romans 10:1

I pray that out of his glorious riches he may strengthen you with power through his Spirit in your inner being.   Ephesians 3:16

Suggested Activity: List a few things you know about your neighbor's spiritual background. Ask God for ways you can be part of His plan for their growth.

Pray for Your Neighbor's Health and Physical Needs (10 Minutes): Lift up any known or unknown needs—health, finances, work, or family, healing for physical or emotional pain, provision for financial or relational needs, wisdom and favor in their daily life:

And my God will meet all your needs according to the riches of his glory in Christ Jesus.

Philippians 4:19

Heal me, LORD, and I will be healed; save me and I will be saved, for you are the one I praise.

Jeremiah 17:14

Suggested Activity: Walk around your neighborhood and quietly pray as you pass your neighbor's home.

Pray for Your Neighbor's Protection and Peace (10 Minutes): Ask God to cover your neighbor with protection and peace in every area of life—protection over their home, children, job, and mental health—and that God's peace would reign in their household and they would have freedom from fear, anxiety, or conflict:

The LORD will keep you from all harm—he will watch over your life.

Psalm 121:7

And the peace of God, which transcends all under-standing, will guard your hearts and your minds in Christ Jesus. Philippians 4:7

Bless Their Relationships and Purpose (10 Minutes): Pray for their relationships—with family, coworkers, and God, that their relationships would be healthy, kind, and supportive, and for reconciliation where needed. Also pray for their life's purpose, that they would walk in their calling and know they have purpose:

If it is possible, as far as it depends on you, live at peace with everyone. Romans 12:18

For we are God's handiwork, created in Christ Jesus to do good works. Ephesians 2:10

Suggested Activity: Send your neighbor a simple message of encouragement (a text or a handwritten note), letting them know you're thinking of them and wishing them well.

Listen, Journal, and Declare Blessings (10 Minutes): Take time to listen to what God may be saying and speak blessings over your neighbor. Ask the Holy Spirit to show you how to love and serve them better. Declare God's blessing over their home and future. Commit your neighbor into God's care:

The LORD bless you and keep you; the LORD make his face shine on you and be gracious to you.

Numbers 6:24-25

Suggested Activity: Journal anything God brings to your heart—words, impressions, scriptures—and end by praying out loud (or in your heart) a blessing over your neighbor.

— PRAYING WHEN YOU CAN'T MAKE ENDS MEET FINANCIALLY —

Preparation (5 Minutes): Begin with a moment of silence. Close your eyes and focus on your dependence on God as your All-in-All, inviting His presence into the moment:

Heavenly Father, I come before You with a heavy heart. I trust in Your provision, even when times are hard. Please give me peace and guidance.

Read the Word (10 Minutes): Read the following scriptures and meditate on their message:

And my God will meet all your needs according to the riches of his glory in Christ Jesus.

Philippians 4:19

So do not worry, saying, "What shall we eat?" or "What shall we drink?" or "What shall we wear?" For the pagans run after all these things, and your heavenly Father knows that you need them. But seek first his kingdom and his righteousness, and all these things will be given to you as well. Therefore, do not worry about tomorrow, for tomorrow will worry about itself. Each day has enough trouble of its own. Matthew 6:31-34

The LORD is my shepherd, I lack nothing.
Psalm 23:1

Reflection and Appreciation (10 Minutes): Write down or say aloud three things you are grateful for, even during this challenging time. Reflect on God's faithfulness in the past and how He has provided for you before.

Petitions and Intercessions (15 Minutes): Share your burdens with God. Be specific about your financial struggles and ask for wisdom and provision.

Lord, you know my needs even before I speak them. I pray for wisdom in managing my resources, for unexpected blessings, and for strength to persevere. Help me to trust You fully, even when I cannot see a way forward.

Pray for others who may also be struggling financially, asking for their needs to be met.

Faith in Action (10 Minutes): Use this time to do something tangible, like listing your financial priorities or seeking one small way to save or earn income. Alternatively, consider setting aside any amount, however small, to donate to someone in greater need, as a step of faith and generosity.

Closing Worship and Affirmations (5 Minutes): End your prayer with a song or hymn that uplifts your spirit, such as "Great is Thy Faithfulness" or "Way Maker." If you prefer, you can simply listen to worship music.

Recite affirmations based on scripture, such as:

"The Lord is my Provider, and I will not fear."

"God is faithful and will supply all my needs."

Final Blessing (5 Minutes):

Lord, thank You for this time of prayer and for hearing my cries. I trust that You are working all things together for my good. Help me to walk in faith, knowing You are my Provider. Amen!

— PRAYING WHEN YOU CAN'T HEAR FROM GOD —

Acknowledge the Silence (10 Minutes):

How long, LORD? Will you forget me forever?
How long will you hide your face from me?

Psalm 13:1

Tell God honestly how you feel. Don't hold back. Acknowledge the silence, confusion, or frustration.

Suggested Activity: Journal your thoughts or write a letter to God starting with, "God, I don't understand…"

Remember God's Faithfulness (10 Minutes):

Yet this I call to mind and therefore I have hope: because of the LORD's great love we are not consumed, for his compassions never fail. They are new every morning; great is your faithfulness.

Lamentations 3:21-23

Recall times when God has been faithful in the past. Thank Him for specific past moments when He answered or comforted you.

Suggested Activity: Make a "God Has Been Faithful" list. Write down as many past blessings or prayers as you can remember. This will inspire your faith for a current need.

Confess and Surrender (10 Minutes):

Search me, God, and know my heart ... . See if there is any offensive way in me and lead me in the way everlasting. Psalm 139:23-24

Ask the Holy Spirit to reveal any sin or distraction that might be creating distance between you and God. Confess anything that comes to mind and surrender control back to God.

Suggested Activity: Sit in silence with open hands. Visualize laying down your worries, sins, or expectations at Jesus' feet.

Wait and Listen (10 Minutes):

Be still and know that I am God.   Psalm 46:10

Instead of talking, practice being silent in God's presence. Welcome His presence without demanding answers.

Suggested Activity: Sit quietly, focusing on your breathing. Every time your mind wanders, gently return to the phrase: "Speak, Lord, Your servant is listening."

Renew Your Trust (10 Minutes):

Trust in the LORD with all your heart and lean not on your own understanding; in all your ways submit to him, and he will make your paths straight.
                                        Proverbs 3:5-6

Affirm your trust in God—even when you don't understand. Ask for the faith to keep walking, even in the dark.

Suggested Activity: Pray or sing a worship song that centers on trust (e.g., "I Trust in God, My Savior," "Way Maker," etc.").

Hope in God's Timing (10 Minutes):

But those who wait on the LORD shall renew their strength... . Isaiah 40:31, NKJV

Close by asking God to renew your strength while you wait. Recommit to seeking Him daily, no matter what. Write down one small daily habit (e.g., five minutes of prayer or Scripture reading) that would help you stay close to God in this season.

— PRAYING AGAINST A REBELLIOUS SPIRIT —

Preparation (5 Minutes): Find a quiet place where you can focus without distractions. Begin with a prayer inviting the Holy Spirit to guide your time of prayer.

Adoration and Worship (10 Minutes):

Come, let us bow down in worship, let us kneel before the LORD our Maker; for He is our God, and we are the people of his pasture, the flock under his care. Psalm 95:6-7

Suggested Activity: Spend time worshiping God through songs, hymns, or simply speaking words of adoration. Acknowledge His sovereignty and goodness.

Confession and Repentance (10 Minutes):

Create in me a pure heart, O God,
  and renew a steadfast spirit within me.
Do not cast me from your presence
  or take your Holy Spirit from me.
Restore to me the joy of your salvation
  and grant me a willing spirit, to sustain me.

Psalm 51:10-12

Suggested Activity: Confess any areas of rebellion or disobedience in your life. Ask God for forgiveness and a renewed heart.

Prayers Against Rebellion (20 Minutes):

Submit yourselves, then, to God. Resist the devil, and he will flee from you.   James 4:7

Acknowledge God's sovereignty and authority over your life. Repent of any rebellious thoughts, actions, or attitudes that have taken root in your heart.

Renounce the spirit of rebellion and surrender your will fully to the will of God.

For rebellion is like the sin of divination, and arrogance like the evil of idolatry. 1 Samuel 15:23

Reject rebellion and arrogance and ask for forgiveness and cleansing. Purify your heart and ask God to renew your spirit, so you can walk in obedience to His commands.

Bind the spirit of rebellion in the name of Jesus and declare that it has no power or authority over you, your family, or your household.

Submit yourselves, then, to God. Resist the devil, and he will flee from you. James 4:7

Submit yourself to God and resist the enemy's attempts to sow rebellion in your life and the lives of family and friends.

Plead the blood of Jesus over your mind, heart, and spirit. Let the protection of God surround you and guard you against the influence of rebellion:

For our struggle is not against flesh and blood, but against the rulers, against the authorities, against the powers of this dark world and against the spiritual forces of evil in the heavenly realms.

Ephesians 6:12

Stand firm in the armor of God, declaring victory over the spirit of rebellion.

Suggested Activity: Pray specific prayers against the spirit of rebellion:

Rise up against bitterness, stubbornness, indisciplined living, non-conformity and lack of self-control. Take authority over questioning of authority, opposition, and disruption.

Release Humility: "Lord, I humble myself before You. Remove any pride or stubbornness from my heart."

Release Obedience: "Father, help me to submit to Your will and follow Your commands."

Release Deliverance: "In the name of Jesus, I break any stronghold of rebellion in my life."

Intercession (10 Minutes): The human spirit has an innate capacity for rebellion, a fiery force that challenges the status quo and pushes boundaries:

For rebellion is like the sin of divination, and arrogance like the evil of idolatry.   1 Samuel 15:23

Silence the voice of rebellion in the human spirit in the name of Jesus. Cut off every root of rebellion. Terminate every demonic influence behind rebellion. Call on fire from Heaven to consume every symptom of rebellion and every plan of the enemy.

Suggested Activity: Pray for others who may be struggling with rebellion. Intercede for family members, friends, and communities.

Thanksgiving and Closing (5 Minutes):

Give thanks in all circumstances; for this is God's will for you in Christ Jesus.   1 Thessalonians 5:18

Suggested Activity: Thank God for hearing your prayers and for His faithfulness. Close with a prayer of gratitude.

Additional Suggested Activities:

JOURNALING: Write down any insights or revelations you receive during your prayer time.

MEDITATION: Spend a few minutes meditating on the scriptures you read.

REFLECTION: Reflect on how you can apply these prayers and scriptures to your daily life.

— PRAYING FOR SEPARATED SPOUSES —

Surrender and Seeking God's Presence (10 Minutes):

The LORD is close to the brokenhearted and saves those who are crushed in spirit. Psalm 34:18

Acknowledge your pain and surrender your emotions to God. Ask Him to fill you with His peace and presence.

Suggested Activity: Play soft worship music and meditate on God's love for you.

Repentance and Healing (10 Minutes):

If we confess our sins, He is faithful and just and will forgive us our sins and purify us from all unrighteousness. 1 John 1:9, NKJV

Confess any personal shortcomings, bitterness, or unforgiveness. Ask God to heal your heart and renew your spirit.

Suggested Activity: Write down any lingering hurts or offenses, and then pray over them, asking God to cleanse your heart.

Intercession for Your Spouse (10 Minutes):

Be kind and compassionate to one another, forgiving each other, just as in Christ God forgave you.

Ephesians 4:32

Pray for your spouse's well-being, spiritual growth, and emotional healing. Ask God to work in their heart and guide them.

Suggested Activity: Speak blessings over your spouse, declaring God's promises over their life.

Restoration and Reconciliation (10 Minutes):

I will restore to you the years that the swarming locust has eaten.   Joel 2:25, NKJV

Ask God to restore what has been broken in your marriage. Pray for wisdom, patience, and divine intervention.

Suggested Activity: Write a letter to God, expressing your hopes for reconciliation and trusting Him with the outcome.

Spiritual Warfare and Protection (10 Minutes):

For our struggle is not against flesh and blood, but against the rulers, against the authorities, against the powers of this dark world.   Ephesians 6:12

Rebuke any spiritual attacks against your marriage, and declare God's protection over your relationship.

Suggested Activity: Speak aloud declarations of faith, such as "My marriage is covered by the blood of Jesus."

Thanksgiving and Trust in God's Plan (10 Minutes):

Do not be anxious about anything, but in every situation, by prayer and petition, with thanksgiving, present your requests to God.

Philippians 4:6

Thank God for His faithfulness and love and for the work He is doing in your life and marriage.

Suggested Activity: End with praise and worship, singing or journaling about God's goodness.

OTHER BOOKS
BY
APOSTLE JACKIE HAREWOOD

Ballistic Apostolic Prayer
(978-1-940461-55-7)

Generational Curses and How to Be Free from Them
(978-1-940461-79-3)

*Intercession Builds Bridges: Frequently Asked Questions
About Intercession*
(978-1-59872-909-2)

Learning to Use Your Greatest Weapon
(978-1-940461-56-4)

*Sing Unto the Lord a New Song: An Introduction to
Praise and Worship*
(0-97-9712623-0-6)

Make a Joyful Noise
(978-1-940461-74-8)

Overshadowed by the Almighty
(978-1-934769-99-7)

Praying Prophetic Prayers
(978-1-950398-52-2)

The Violent Take It by Force
(978-1-934769-11-9)

Warring with the Scriptures
(978-1-940461-73-1)

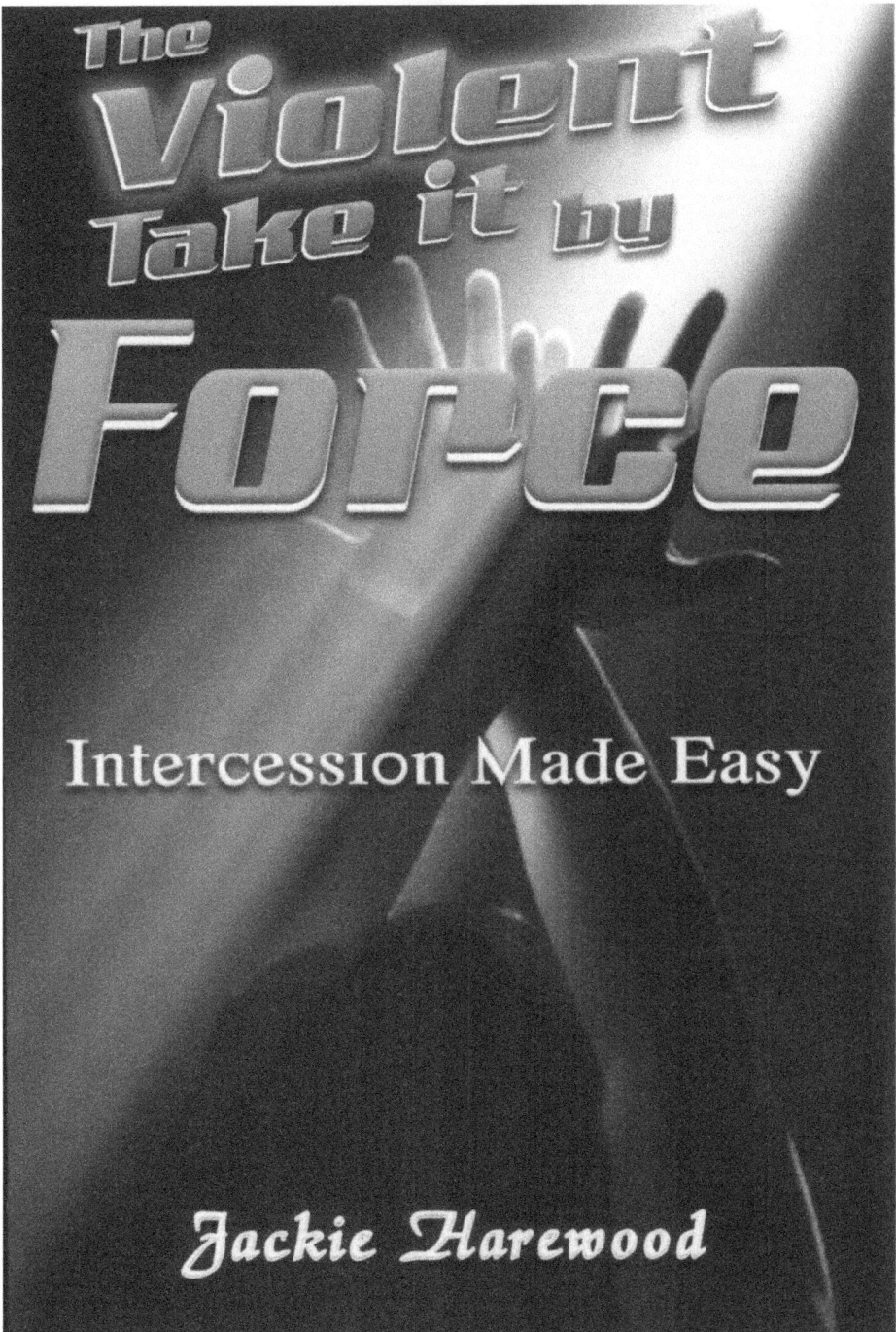

The Violent Take it by Force

Intercession Made Easy

Jackie Harewood

Overshadowed
by the Almighty

Understanding
the Phenomenon
Known as
"Being Slain
in the Spirit"

With a special
chapter entitled
What Does God's Voice
Sound Like?

Prophetess Jackie Harewood

Ballistic

Apostolic

Prayer

Jackie Harewood

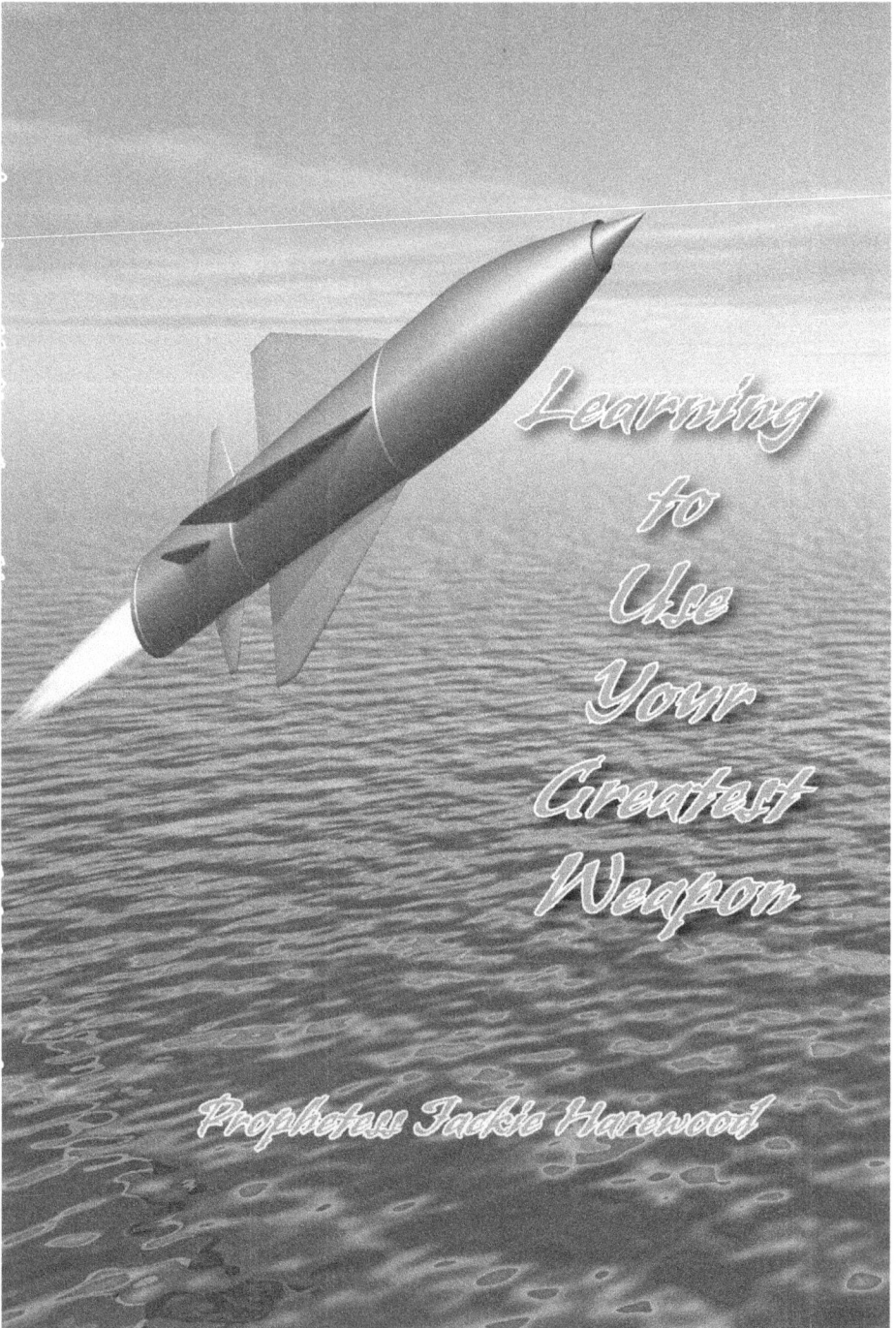

Learning to Use Your Greatest Weapon

Prophetess Jackie Harewood

WARRING with the SCRIPTURES

Arm Yourself with Power-Packed Words to Reign in Victory

Prophetess Jackie Harewood

MAKE A JOYFUL NOISE

An Introduction to Praise and Worship

**Prophetess
Jackie
Harewood**

GENERATIONAL CURSES

AND HOW TO BE FREE FROM THEM

Prophetess Jackie Harewood

PRAYING PROPHETIC PRAYERS

PROPHETESS JACKIE HAREWOOD

AUTHOR CONTACT PAGE

Apostle Jackie Harewood
37041 Agnes Webb Avenue
Prairieville, LA 70769

jharewoodla@cox.net
(225) 772-4552